FRUITY PASSIONS

*Margaret Vaughan
and Mary Hardiman-Jones*

BBC Books

PROGRAMME CREDITS

The BBC TV *Fruity Passions* series was produced and directed by Andy Kemp and first broadcast in 1990. The series was presented by Margaret Vaughan; the Associate Producer was Mary Hardiman-Jones.

MARGARET VAUGHAN

Margaret Vaughan was born into a large farming family in Scotland and later herself married a farmer and became a shepherdess, first in Shropshire and then in Somerset where she brought up her two children. But it was not until 1973, when she started preparing lunches at a local pub, that she realised where her mother's tuition in traditional farmhouse cookery could lead her. In 1975 she opened The Settle restaurant in Frome and, later, her own bakery. She now combines running this successful business, which has been commended by Egon Ronay, with her new broadcasting career.

MARY HARDIMAN-JONES

Mary Hardiman-Jones trained at the Central School of Speech and Drama and worked for Devon's Education Service before becoming one of the original team of producers with BBC Radio Devon. She has since worked on *Woman's Hour*, *You & Yours* and other Radio 4 programmes and is now a producer with BBC Television. Mary has lived in the heart of the Devon countryside for some years and it was the abundant produce of a large garden that kindled her interest in country winemaking. She carried out the original research for the *Fruity Passions* series and co-authored the Introduction to this book.

Published by BBC Books,
a division of BBC Enterprises Limited,
Woodlands, 80 Wood Lane, London W12 0TT
First published 1990
Reprinted 1990 (twice), 1992

Set in 12/13 pt Caslon by Goodfellow and Egan
Printed by Clays Ltd, St Ives plc
Cover printed by Clays Ltd, St Ives plc

CONTENTS

ACKNOWLEDGEMENTS

My sincere thanks to everyone who has contributed in so many ways in helping me to write this book, with prayers, and by sharing their recipes, experiences and, of course, their wines.

To my family for their loving encouragement, my staff at The Settle Restaurant and Bakehouse for their support.

To Andy Kemp for his sure guidance and endless patience. To Carol Mattison for ironing out most of the problems.

To Tom Stewart for his tolerance at my inability to conquer the wordprocessor, so leaving him to do most of the typing.

To Mary Hardiman-Jones for her invaluable research and contribution, and to her husband Terry for helping and encouraging her.

And to Jennie Allen at BBC Books and Wendy Hobson for those dreaded deadlines without which I would never have finished.

                                    Margaret Vaughan

PREFACE

The BBC asked me to write a book to accompany the *Fruity Passions* television series and of course, in a moment of weakness, I agreed. It sounded a splendid idea – a golden opportunity to share some of my favourite recipes with you. So how can I get across to you the fun of making and tasting your own country wines? The written word does not come easily to me, so forgive me if I digress now and again into my little world of memories and anecdotes. After all is said and drunk, these tales are an enjoyable part of this great hobby of winemaking.

Many friends have, over the years, contributed to my store of recipes, sharing tips and tipples, best vintages and failures, heartaches and headaches – but then, isn't that what friends are for? I only wish I could remember all their names. Some will stay with me for ever, like that of Ted, our local blacksmith who, forty years ago, gave me my very own stein with a tap. I still have it and use it to make the oak leaf wine that Mrs Wigley taught me. How appropriate that I now call it 'Wigley Oak Leaf Wine' – not that the leaves are any more convoluted than usual, just that your legs are after a glass or two!

You see? I digress already, but that's how it is when you start country winemaking because the fun of it is quite intoxicating. I can see I am going to enjoy sharing the picking and the plucking, the plunging and the pressing, the bubbling and the bottling, straining and sieving, waiting and wondering – and best of all, hopefully, helping you to achieve something worthwhile at very little cost.

If, on the way, I can persuade some of you to join my passionate crusade to preserve and enjoy our wonderful heritage of hedgerows and country goodness, I shall certainly be raising my glass.

Margaret Vaughan

CONVERSION TABLES

All these are approximate conversions which have been rounded either up or down. In a few recipes it has been necessary to modify them very slightly. Never mix metric and imperial measures in one recipe. Stick to one system or the other.

Teaspoon and tablespoon measures are level, not heaped.

WEIGHTS	VOLUME
¼ oz (10 g)	1 fl oz (25 ml)
½ oz (15 g)	2 fl oz (50 ml)
1 oz (25 g)	4 fl oz (120 ml)
2 oz (50 g)	¼ pint (150 ml)
8 oz (225 g)	8 fl oz (250 ml)
1 lb (450 g)	½ pint (300 ml)
1 ½ lb (750 g)	1 pint (600 ml)
2 lb (1 kg)	1½ pints (900 ml)
2 ½ lb (1.25 kg)	2 pints (1.2 l)
3 lb (1.5 kg)	3 pints (1.75 l)
3 ½ lb (1.5 kg)	4 pints (2.25 l)
4 lb (1.75 kg)	5 pints (2.75 l)
4 ½ lb (2 kg)	6 pints (3.4 l)
5 lb (2.25 kg)	7 pints (3.9 l)
5 ½ lb (2.5 kg)	8 pints (4.5 l)
6 lb (2.75 kg)	2 gallons (9 l)
	3 gallons (13.5 l)
	4 gallons (18 l)
	5 gallons (23 l)
	6 gallons (27 l)

NOTES ON THE RECIPES

You should find that the recipes in this book are simplicity itself to make from country ingredients, using tried-and-tested methods. All the details of equipment and processes are given in the first section of the book, and these general reminders will help you make your own delicious wines.

- *All the recipes are for 1 gallon (4.5 l) of wine.*
- *Always start by sterilising all your equipment, otherwise you could ruin your wine.*
- *Measure pints (litres) of flower heads or other produce by placing them in a large measuring jug or a bowl of which you know the capacity, and pressing them down very gently.*
- *Wash all fruits, flowers and vegetables before use.*
- *Sultanas or raisins should be soaked in several changes of hot water, then drained.*
- *Unless the recipe is specific, use ordinary granulated sugar. You can, of course, experiment with others, but remember that brown sugars will alter the colour and taste of the wine.*
- *Where boiling is indicated, simmer gently and avoid vigorous boiling.*
- *It is best to start the yeast working before adding it to the rest of the ingredients. Simply rehydrate the sachet of yeast by mixing it with a little warm water. Leave it for 5 minutes before adding it to the lukewarm must in the fermentation bucket.*
- *Make sure that you cover the fermentation bucket and seal the demijohns carefully to keep out wine-flies or airborne bacteria that could spoil the wine.*

- *Store fermentation buckets or wine fermenting in demijohns in a warm room, but nowhere too hot. Once siphoned into storage jars or bottled, store in a cool dark place with as constant a temperature as possible.*
- *Keep the airlock topped up with sulphite solution.*
- *You will know that fermentation is complete when the bubbles of carbon dioxide stop blipping through the airlock.*
- *Top up demijohns with cooled boiled water after siphoning off to maintain the quantity of wine.*

Never pick rare or protected wild flowers, however prolific they may seem to be in your granny's old wine book. Cowslips are an obvious example – the countryside used to be full of them but now they are very rare. Stick to dandelions, elderflowers or honeysuckle in the wild or choose roses from the garden.

· 1 ·
ROSE-COLOURED GLASSES

In making the BBC television series *Fruity Passions*, we have heard many a nostalgic tale about country winemaking in Britain. The picture so often painted is of a grandmother or an aunt in the country, who made wines with each season of the year as regularly as she made jam, pickles or Christmas puddings.

By the height of summer, the great bowls of fermenting fruit were slowly bubbling in the kitchen, on a stone slab in the larder or in the cool of the farm dairy. Each bowl or 'wine crock' was covered with butter muslin, and an inquisitive youngster peering underneath would see a piece of toast spread with bakers' or brewers' yeast, floating on top of the fruity mixture.

The method was simplicity itself. The yeast grew through the bread, feeding on the fruit and sugar, until quite a crust formed across the top. This was carefully lifted off and thrown to the chickens, then the wine was slowly poured into a stone cask or jar to mature. There were no demijohns, no fancy filters or sophisticated wine yeasts.

The wine was left for at least a year, preferably in the cellar, and a suitable brew was chosen for special celebrations. Elderflower or gooseberry 'Champagne' was light and fragrant for summer drinking, but many others were rich and sweet, more like sherry or port. 'A drop of wine' was offered to guests or callers much as tea or coffee are offered today.

In winter, there was rich sloe wine to keep out the cold or mulled elderberry 'rob' for Christmas visitors. Dandelion and parsley wines were popular as spring tonics and others were taken for coughs and colds or as a nightcap. Parsnip or peapod wine, damson 'port' or carrot 'whisky' – each wine had its curative properties and its place in the country calendar.

For many families, country wines were not just a way of providing home-made remedies or inexpensive hospitality, they were an obvious way of using up surplus produce – 'waste not, want not'. Any smallholder or keen gardener will know that situation when you say, 'There must be *something* else we can do with all this fruit'.

When it came to making the wines, this was often a social occasion, too, with family and friends of all ages roped in to help pick the flowers or fruit. At the end of the day, it was time to try last year's bottles of the same wine, or perhaps even an older vintage for a special celebration.

But that's enough nostalgia for the time being. Today, we lead busy lives juggling work and family commitments, and there's precious little time left over for making wine. Few of us have large cool larders in our kitchens for storing great quantities of wine but the cupboard under the stairs is quite adequate. Many of us, too, are town-dwellers, so collecting the ingredients takes that bit more effort involved in a trip to the country.

The doctor can prescribe all manner of sophisticated drugs for common ailments, where grandmother would have given a tot of elderberry or an eggcupful of dandelion. The social traditions have changed, too. Sadly, most people are far too busy to call round and pass the time of day over a glass of wine.

So why bother to make wine today? There are lots of reasons – and the first and foremost is that it is *fun*; the fun of learning and the sense of achievement. At first you'll be pleased to produce anything that's drinkable, but later you'll be learning how to adapt recipes, blending to suit your own taste. It can be utterly absorbing.

Second, it's *inexpensive* fun. Wines made from flowers and fruits from your own garden, or from the hedgerows cost very little – just the price of the sugar and a little yeast in many cases. Even if you haven't a window-box, let alone a garden, you can still pick elderflowers and blackberries for free. Then you can buy bargain boxes of fruit or vegetables when there is a glut in the market. The basic equipment will cost under £10. Also, when you realise how much duty you pay on commercial wine, it's quite an incentive to try making your own.

Third, you will *know what you're drinking*. There is no need to use chemical additives in winemaking; the recipes in this book do not. You can stick to the simplest tried-and-tested methods and make delicious, wholesome country wines. There is plenty of choice, too. You can choose whether to make a strong after-dinner wine, a light low-alcohol one or a cordial. You can experiment with wines which are quick to mature and others which need a bit more patience to give of their best.

Perhaps this is where I should mention my fears over today's updated winemaking methods. They may be a little more scientific and therefore one would perhaps expect fewer failures; but are we in danger of creating homogenised wines – all tasting almost alike? Nature does not give us perfect sowing, growing and harvesting conditions every single year, neither does every garden, hedgerow, field or forest have perfect soil, so of course our wines should taste different from county to county. Each region has its own particular speciality which should come through in the flavour and bouquet of our country wines. Of course use modern techniques if you so wish, but the best wines are made using natural ingredients, simple methods, patience and care. The only concession I make is to use the new wine yeasts which are very good indeed.

And lastly, even if you make a few mistakes, you will have moments of great pride. When you share a special wine that you have made, you have not only the satisfaction of serving your very own vintage, but also the knowledge that you are helping to keep alive a centuries-old British tradition.

Those anxious to get on and make their first bottles of wine, will probably want to rush out and buy a few items of basic equipment. But first, a thought or two about the end product.

ALCOHOL – SOME MYTHS AND A SOBERING THOUGHT

Even if you have never made or tasted any country wines, you will surely have heard tales about their supposed powers. The vet who was persuaded to take a tot from the farmer and was later found sinking under the table, the respectable 'townie' who happily swigs back several fruity concoctions in the village and then can't walk in a straight line – our television comedies are full of them. But are the old-fashioned wines always so potent?

It is, of course, the combination of yeast and sugar that gives the wine its alcoholic strength, so country wines are potentially no more lethal than any others. 'Everything in moderation' applies well here. If you load bags of sugar into your brewing bucket, use a surfeit of fruit 'to give it more taste' (although you will probably ruin the taste) and then serve it in your largest glasses, you have only yourself to blame!

Some of the wines our grandparents made were sweeter and stronger. They were often fortified with brandy (spirits were cheaper then!) and were served in small glasses as a winter warmer or a nightcap – much better for you than sleeping tablets. Do not, then, follow one of granny's winter recipes if you want to produce a light 'quaffing' wine to drink in the garden, or a dry little number to go with the fish course.

In contrast to the comedy stereotypes, many of the real country winemakers are not heavy drinkers at all. Some are virtually teetotal and take the greatest pleasure in giving their bottles away. It seems that even very low-alcohol wines can give you another kind of lift – that of uncorking and sharing something that you have made yourself for next-to-nothing and the realisation that it tastes good.

One more note of caution. Hopefully, you will be so proud of your wines that, like generations of country people, you will want to share them. You may even enter a bottle or two in a local show. But don't be tempted to take them to the annual bazaar or fête as it is illegal to sell any wines without a Customs and Excise licence.

That's the end of the lesson. Now, let's get going!

·2·

GETTING STARTED – EQUIPMENT

If you are new to winemaking, don't rush out to buy six demijohns and make as many different wines in the first month. Just make 1 gallon (4.5 l) of a simple wine and tend it carefully through the various stages up to bottling. Then, when your first precious batch is made, try a gallon of something different. You may not end up with a cellar full of bottles at the end of the first year, but those you have are much more likely to be drinkable.

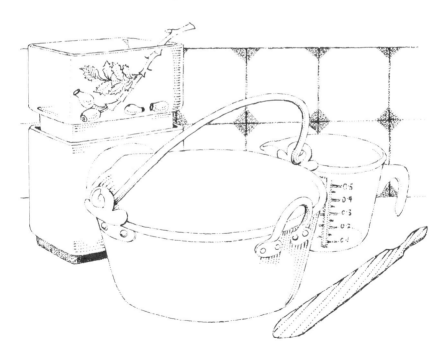

You will probably find that you already have much of the equipment you need in your kitchen. You don't need a lot of room, either, although if winemaking really takes hold of you, the garage or spare bedroom might well become your private winery! In the days when most houses had sculleries or outhouses (with the 'copper' in the corner for boiling the washing) this was the ideal place, but a kitchen worktop near a sink will do just as well.

Here is the basic equipment you will need for your first batch of wine. If you do not have suitable items in your kitchen, you can buy all these at a chemist's or home-brew shop, or you may even find them second hand.

PREPARING THE INGREDIENTS

As well as your main ingredients, sugar and yeast, of course, you may need your kitchen scales and measuring jug. For recipes in which you boil ingredients, you will need a large saucepan or preserving pan, preferably with a non-stick, enamel or stainless steel surface. Avoid brass, copper or cast iron pans as these metals can taint your wine. You will also need a long-handled plastic or wooden spoon.

STERILISING

For sterilising I use Campden tablets (made from sodium metabisulphite), but there are other sterilising agents available. Simply dissolve the tablets in water to form a sulphite solution. A bottle-brush will make it easier to get bottles and demijohns really clean.

FERMENTING ON THE PULP

A 2-gallon (9-litre) white or colourless fermentation bucket with a lid is ideal for starting off the fermentation of the fruit, sugar and yeast. You can buy larger ones, but they are very heavy when filled with liquid. Do not use a coloured plastic bucket as the colour can react with the acid in your wine and make it poisonous. You may be lucky enough to have a glazed earthenware or stoneware bowl –

called a wine crock or stein. Some of these have wooden lids, but you can use large clean cloths, polythene or cling film. Never leave wine to stand for any length of time in a metal container, as the acid in the wine can dissolve the metal.

STRAINING

A large (about 8 in (20 cm)) funnel and large nylon sieve or straining bag are used to strain the liquid into a demijohn.

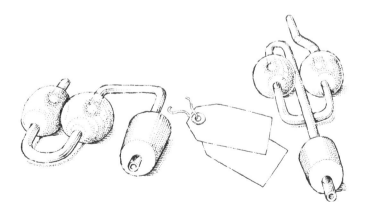

FERMENTATION

A clear glass 1-gallon (4.5-l) demijohn or fermentation jar is needed next, with a rubber bung with a hole in it, to fit in the top of the jar and a glass or plastic airlock to fit into the bung. The airlock is filled with cooled boiled water. Have a tie-on parcel label handy on which to make a note of your ingredients.

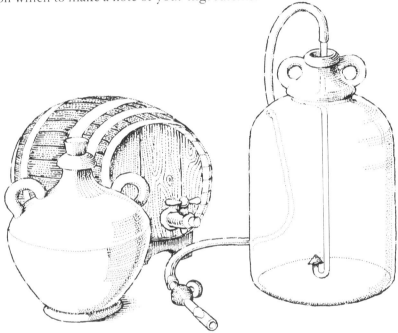

SIPHONING

Siphoning or 'racking off' mean the same thing. You will need a second demijohn or an empty cider jar, large spirit bottle or small sherry cask, as well as a solid rubber bung to seal the vessel. Some winemakers use stone or earthenware storage jars. To siphon the liquid from one jar to the other, you will need a transparent plastic siphon tube about 4 feet (1.2 m) long. Most have a 'J' tube or some device at one end for keeping the end of the tube above the sediment; some have a tap at the other.

STORING AND BOTTLING

You may decide to store your wine in the demijohns or earthenware storage jars instead of bottling it, which saves time and space. Some of these have taps so that you can draw some wine off and check the colour and clarity; but if not, simply use a pipette (also known as a 'wine thief') to take out a sample.

If you prefer to bottle it up, start saving bottles – six for 1 gallon (4.5 l) – clear, pale green or brown for white wine and dark green for red, and buy a packet of corks and a simple corking tool. Plastic corks are OK, but may be difficult to remove. Flanged corks are not suitable if you are going to lay down your bottles as they are more likely to leak. Always label your wine bottles. Any stick-on labels will do, but you may like to buy some attractive wine labels, draw your own, or even have some printed.

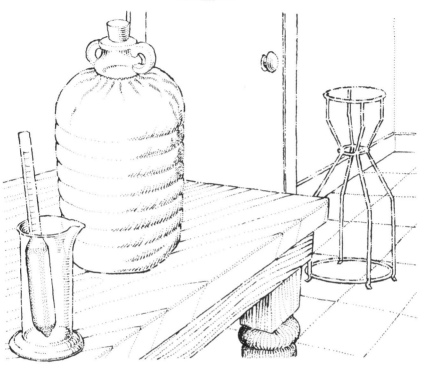

EXTRAS

Home-brew shops are full of all manner of gadgets which may be intriguing but are by no means necessary. It is generally better not to buy unless you are convinced that the simplest method is not the best. For example, you can buy a plastic-covered metal frame which sits on top of a demijohn with a straining bag suspended over a funnel to help you strain fruit into the fermentation jar. You can buy all manner of filters or fruit-crushers, and even an electrically-heated jacket to keep your fermentation jar warm in winter! Some people may tell you to buy a hydrometer and jar so that you can measure the specific gravity of your wine (see p. 39), but you can make delicious wine without one.

STERILISING

The most common cause of home-made wines 'going wrong' is contamination from one of the many kinds of bacteria that are lurking around the cleanest of houses. The worst culprit is the vinegar bacteria, *Mycoderma aceti*, which is airborne or carried by the fruit- or vinegar-fly. It literally turns wine into wine vinegar. The answer is first to wash and then sterilise all your equipment properly.

Dissolve two Campden tablets in 1 pint (600 ml) of water in your fermentation bucket. Put on the lid and swirl the water round to sterilise the inside. Wash all the equipment that you will be using in the solution in the bucket and then leave it to drain.

It is a good idea to leave about 1 in (2.5 cm) of this sulphite solution in demijohns that you are storing for some time. This kills off any bacteria in the air in the jars.

When preparing bottles, clean them carefully with a bottle-brush, then immerse them in sulphite solution, making sure there are no air bubbles trapped inside, and leave them to soak for a short while before you use them.

· 4 ·

THE MAGIC OF YEAST

Before making up your first batch of wine, it is worth knowing a little about how the fermentation process works. Yeast is the 'magic' ingredient in winemaking. Without it, there would be no fermentation and therefore no alcohol. Just as yeast grows and gives life to the dough for bread, so it does to the unfermented juice in winemaking. Perhaps we should say 'they' instead of 'it', because 'yeast' really means millions of microscopic, single-cell plants.

For centuries, winemakers relied on the natural wild yeasts that are present on most fruits and flowers, or they used bakers' or brewers' yeast to ferment their wines. The most common method was to spread some yeast on a piece of toast and float this on the top of the must, the mixture of fruit or flowers and sugar.

Now, however, we have yeasts specifically selected and cultivated to give the best strains for winemaking, and they are very good indeed. They are most likely to give the best flavour, a higher alcohol level and leave a solid sediment so that you can easily siphon off the wine from the 'lees'. They are generally labelled 'general wine yeast' or 'suitable for dry white wines' and are sold in dehydrated form in foil packets, which you can store in the fridge to keep them fresh. You may see different specialised kinds of yeast such as 'Sauterne', 'Burgundy' or 'Bordeaux style', but since your own personal country wines are what you are after, you don't need these. It is also best to avoid the larger jars or drums of yeast mixed with yeast nutrients since these deteriorate quickly.

To use the sachets, all you need to do is rehydrate the yeast by mixing it with a little warm water and leave it for about 5 minutes, then add it to the wine mixture. *This is called starting the yeast.*

What happens then is that the yeast cells begin to multiply. Given an ideal temperature of about 55–65°F (13–18°C) for white wine or 65–75°F (18–24°C) for red, the cells start to feed on the fruit and sugar mixture, growing and dividing. In doing so, they give off equal amounts of alcohol and carbon gas dioxide gas – the process known as fermentation. You know that the mixture is fermenting because the carbon dioxide gas bubbles through the solution in the airlock. Fermentation will continue until either the yeast has 'eaten up' all the sugar (in which case the wine will taste dry) or the alcohol level has risen to its limit – somewhere between 9 per cent and 18 per cent by volume is when the yeast cells die. The dead cells sink to the bottom of the bucket or demijohn as a thick layer of sediment known as the 'lees'.

You may see yeast nutrients or vitamin B_1, thiamin, in home-brew shops. These are designed to help the yeast to grow, but are generally only required in a few of the recipes since the natural ingredients provide all the qualities the yeast needs for most wines.

Finally, remember that piling in a lot of sugar will not automatically produce a strong wine. It may even stop fermentation taking place. So you only need to add the right quantity of sugar, as directed in the recipes, to make a delicious wine.

· 5 ·

YOUR FIRST GALLON OF WINE

A MUST IS A MUST!

To make any wine, you first make up what is called the 'must' (from the Latin word for new), then add the yeast to start it fermenting. The must is basically a mixture of fruit, flowers or leaves to give the wine its flavour, with water, sugar and acid – a real gourmet mixture for your wine yeast, which will make it grow like mad.

The sugar comes from the fruit or fruit juice, as well as the sugar you add from a packet. Obviously, if there is a lot of sweet fruit in the recipe, you won't need to add as much sugar. In mead, of course, the sugar is from honey. Indeed, some of the really old country wine recipes call for honey, since it was formerly far more readily available than sugar. The nutritious and medicinal properties of honey are well known and if you have a good source of

USING THE FREEZER   *One of the great joys of winemaking today is that you can use the freezer both to improve the wine and to help you cope with busy times of the year.*

Instead of making the wine as soon as you have picked the fruit, you can simply wash and freeze it. This means that if you have a glut in the garden, you don't have to turn it all into wine at once. Also, you can make the wine at your leisure – perhaps on a rainy day in February when there's nothing much to do. You don't have to blanch or fast freeze fruit for winemaking. In fact, it's better to freeze it slowly, because the formation of crystals breaks down the fruit and when it thaws it gives off its juice more readily.

it (not the blended kind) you might well consider substituting honey for at least part of the sugar in some recipes: 1 lb (450 g) of honey to 14 oz (400 g) of sugar is about the right ratio.

Acid is also necessary for fermentation. Some fruits contain enough on their own, but if the main ingredient is low in natural acid, the recipe may call for oranges or lemons, which add citric acid as well as flavour or sultanas which add tartaric acid. Citric acid and tartaric acid are also available in powdered form.

Your First Wine

For those of you embarking on your very first wine, we are going to take you stage-by-stage through making Apple Wine. This is a simple and favourite recipe from readily available ingredients, and is a great way to learn and enjoy the basic techniques of wine-making.

When you start on other wines, you will find that different ingredients may require slightly different treatment. But all the necessary information is given in the recipes themselves.

Always sterilise all your equipment before you start (see page 20).

Apple Wine Ingredients

6 lb (2.75 kg) apples
Finely peeled rind and juice of 2
lemons

3 lb (1.5 kg) sugar
8 pints (4.5 l) boiling water
¼ oz (10 g) wine yeast

Apple Wine – Preparing the Must

Wine can be made from all kinds of apples: cookers, eaters, crab-apples and windfalls. In fact, a mixture is usually best. You don't have to peel or core the apples for wine as you do for most chutneys and for cooking, so this is a quick way of making use of a lot of fruit.

Wash the apples and cut away any bruised or damaged parts.

Weigh them, then chop them roughly by hand or use a slicing attachment on a food processor, or a juice extractor.

Place the apples, lemon rind and juice, and the sugar in a fermentation bucket. Pour on the boiling water. Stir until the sugar has dissolved and squash the fruit against the sides of the bucket to break it down. Other recipes may have additional ingredients to add at this stage: sultanas for tartaric acid and flavour, tea for tannin or ginger for flavour. If you are using oranges or lemons, make sure that you do not allow any of the white pith to get into the wine since this will make it very bitter. The amount of sugar in a recipe will depend on the type of fruit or vegetable used, since some are naturally sweeter than others. If you are experimenting with a wine, it is better to err on the side of caution as it is easy to sweeten a wine that is too dry, but difficult to achieve the opposite effect.

Start the yeast by mixing it with a little warm water and leaving it for 5 minutes. Then add it to the lukewarm must.

FERMENTING ON THE PULP

Cover the bucket tightly and leave it in a warm room for about 3 days. Don't consign it to a cold garage or hot airing cupboard; average room temperature is about right. The mixture will start to ferment on the pulp, and the yeast will begin to 'eat into' the fruit and extract both colour and flavour. After a while you will see tiny bubbles of fermentation forming on the surface. Stir the mixture with a sterilised spoon once or twice a day, always replacing the lid afterwards.

STRAINING AND FERMENTATION

After about 3 or 4 days, the mixture is ready to be strained into a 1 gallon (4.5 l) demijohn. Place a large funnel in the demijohn and rest a sieve or straining bag in the funnel. Tip the funnel to one side so that the air can escape from the jar as you fill it, and slowly pour the liquid into the jar. The demijohn should be filled to the bottom of the neck; not too full since fermentation at this stage can be quite fierce and if there is no room, the wine will bubble up into the airlock. If you have too much juice, use it up in a casserole or sauce. Nothing need be wasted. If you don't have quite enough, top up with cooled boiled water.

BLENDING INGREDIENTS *Most country wine recipes concentrate on one main ingredient: apple, elderberry, dandelion. That way, although all wines are individual, you have more control over the finished article. Of course, you will want to use what ingredients are available to you. You may have three different types of apples for your Apple Wine, for example. And there are some well proven examples of wines which blend the qualities of two or three main ingredients to achieve a good balance: Strawberry and Redcurrant, Elderflower and Gooseberry, Rowanberry and Wheat. In general, however, straightforward wines are the best to try first. Save the blending of ingredients until you have a little more practice, and try blending the wines instead – more rewarding, less risky and great fun. You'll find the tips on how to do this in Chapter 8.*

With most wines you can squeeze the bag or press the fruit in the sieve to extract as much juice as possible; one or two recipes, including this apple one, recommend that you do not squeeze the fruit since it may make the wine cloudy. You can use the pulp from the fruit for jam, chutney or in a fruit pie – there are recipes for these in this book too.

Seal the demijohn with an airlock, and half fill the airlock with a little cooled boiled water, keeping this topped up as the wine ferments. Store the demijohn in a warm place (again, not too warm) for about 2 or 3 months until the wine has worked itself out. Fermentation times will vary considerably depending on the ingredients, the temperature and so on. Once the wine has worked itself out, the carbon dioxide will have stopped bubbling through the airlock and a fairly thick sediment of ¼ to ½ in (5 to 10 mm) will be visible at the bottom of the jar.

Always make a note of your ingredients on a tie-on label or a piece of paper, rolled up and tucked into the handle of the demijohn. Then, whether you produce a brilliant wine or a disappointing one, you will know how to repeat (or improve) the recipe.

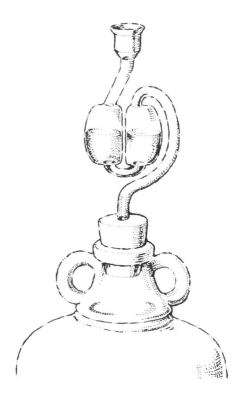

SIPHONING

Once the wine has worked itself out, it is time to siphon off the clearing wine from the lees; this is sometimes called 'racking off'. Don't be too impatient to siphon off the wine since the time any wine takes to ferment will vary depending on the ingredients, the growing season, the weather and where the wine has been stored. Any times indicated in the recipes can only be a guide. Wait until all activity has ceased and the wine is beginning to clear.

For Apple Wine, you only need to siphon off the wine once into a clean demijohn or glass container and seal it with a rubber bung.

With a glass container, you will be able to see the colour and clarity of your wine as it matures. I like to use stoneware or earthenware storage jars as they help to keep the wine cool and dark.

Some winemakers siphon off their wines several times, and each time the wine will become clearer as it throws down a little more sediment. If you want a sparklingly clear wine, then you may wish to siphon at least twice. But a small sediment in a storage jar or bottle does not harm the wine. You may hear that it is not good for the wine to be left on the lees for too long. This is only true in a few cases, and these are clearly indicated in the individual recipes. In fact, we greatly value a sediment in a port or a classic French red wine since it often indicates that the wine has had time to mature to

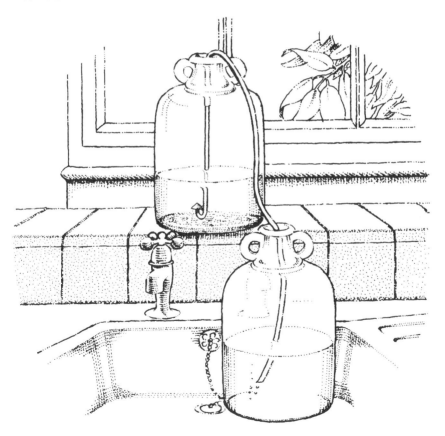

full flavour in the bottle. So there is no reason to be worried about the same thing in our country wines.

If you have a steady hand you may be able to pour the wine through a funnel into a second demijohn, stopping just before you reach the sediment. But for most of us it is easier to siphon with a length of sterilised plastic tubing.

Stand the full demijohn on the draining board and the clean one in the sink, since the empty jar must be at a lower level. Take the airlock and bung out of the first jar and dangle one end of the plastic tube into the wine, keeping the end well clear of the sediment. Most siphon tubes now have a J-shaped device to stop the end entering the sediment. If yours does not, tie a cocktail stick or a small knitting needle to the bottom of the tube with an elastic band to keep the end clear. Put the other end of the tube in your mouth and suck gently until the wine begins to flow down the tube. Quickly take the tube out of your mouth, put it well down into the empty demijohn and the wine will siphon from one jar to the other.

When the level in the top jar has dropped to just above the sediment, stop. Do not be tempted to try to salvage every last drop as you are bound to get some of the sediment in the second jar. Just leave it to settle and use the liquid in gravy, sauces or casseroles. The last drop of sediment can go on the compost heap.

Wash out and sterilise the empty demijohn as soon as possible – it will be a lot easier to clean now than if the sediment is left to dry.

Because you have discarded a little, the wine will not quite fill the second jar. It is important to top up the demijohn since a large airspace in the jar may allow the wine to oxidise or go brown – what's more, you want to end up with the same quantity of wine. Simply top up with cooled boiled water – it will not affect the strength of the finished wine.

Remember that you must sterilise everything at each stage.

TASTING AND ADJUSTING

The siphoning stage is the ideal time to taste your wine and see how it is progressing. The easiest way is to use a small pipette to take out a little of the wine to try. More than anything else, your taste buds will tell you how it is coming along. If it is too sweet or has a yeasty flavour, it may not have finished fermenting. Seal it with an airlock and leave it to ferment a little longer. If you have simply made a very sweet wine, save it for serving with desserts, or try blending it with drier wines (more on this in Chapter 8). If it is too dry, you can try adding a little sugar syrup, then seal with an airlock and allow it to ferment a little longer.

If you are using stoneware or earthenware jars to mature your wine, extracting at this stage also gives you a chance to see the colour and clarity.

MATURING

After siphoning off the Apple Wine, seal the demijohn with a solid rubber bung and leave it in a cool dark place for 2 to 3 months to mature. For a red or rosé wine, either use dark jars or bottles or wrap newspapers round the jars to keep them dark, as exposure to light can bleach the colour and affect the flavour.

Different wines will mature at different rates, some taking as long as a year before they are at their best. The recipes give indications of those which need a particularly long time to mature. Try to be patient, and if you know you will find this difficult, start with a few quicker wines to get you going before you try a long-maturing one. That way you will not be tempted to open them all too quickly.

BOTTLING

You don't have to bottle your wine. It will keep and mature beautifully in demijohns or stone jars, which take up far less space, and you can decant some of the wine when you wish to serve it by either siphoning it off or using a tap fitment. However, if you only want to use small quantities of wine at a time, you may prefer to bottle the wine, since a half-empty jar of wine will oxidise and spoil.

You can use wine bottles over and over again, so start collecting in good time: dark green for red wine, and clear, pale green or brown for white. Some winemakers like to use the type of commercial wine bottle most in keeping with the contents – dark red wine in a Bordeaux bottle, fruity white in a Hock bottle and so on. You will need about six bottles for each gallon (4.5 l), or you may want to bottle up a few half-bottles for convenience.

Stand the demijohn on the draining board, and the clean sterilised bottles in the sink. Start siphoning the wine into the first

bottle, and stop when the wine reaches about 1 in (2.5 cm) up the neck of the bottle as there needs to be a small airspace between the wine and the bottom of the cork. A siphon tube with a tap on the end is handy here, as you can turn off the tap at exactly the right place and transfer the tube into the next bottle. Otherwise simply press your thumb over the end of the tube. As before, be careful not to suck up the sediment from the jar, but stop siphoning just before you reach the bottom. If you have a little wine over, it need never be wasted; you can drink it straight away, or seal it in a smaller bottle and use it in your cooking.

CORKING

Corks need to be soaked before use, so dissolve one Campden tablet in 1 pint (600 ml) of warm water and place the corks in the solution. Use a small plate or bowl to keep them under the surface of the water so that they soak right through.

It is possible to ram the corks home with a wooden mallet, but a simple corking machine is much easier and more efficient. There are two main kinds. One has a lever and a handle to push the cork in. The other is a kind of wooden cylinder. The cork is dropped in and the whole gadget rested over the bottle, so you use a wooden mallet on the wood rather than on fragile cork to drive the cork right home.

You may wish to use a foil or plastic cap over the cork to add the finishing touch. You can buy these from home-brew shops.

LABELLING

Whatever you do, don't think you will remember exactly which wine is in which bottle. Dusty mystery bottles, discovered in years to come at the back of a cupboard, may provide an intriguing guessing game, but 'Elderberry 1985' is much more impressive.

If you are thinking of entering your wine into a competition, there will almost certainly be rules about the kind of bottle, cork and label you should use, so read Chapter 14 and find out the rules before you start.

STORING

Lay the bottles down in a cool dark place for at least 2 months before drinking. Few modern houses have cellars or dark cupboards with stone floors, and in centrally heated houses, the best place might well be at the back of the garage. If you have used straight-sided corks, the bottles need to be on their sides to prevent the corks drying out and letting in air. Bottles with plastic corks can be stood upright, but need checking from time to time as these corks have a habit of rising out of the bottle, especially in warm weather. If this happens, ram them home straight away.

The amount of time you leave your wine to mature in the bottle is up to you and the recipe. Nearly all wines improve with keeping – particularly the reds – and it pays to lay down at least one or two bottles for the longer term, even if you can't resist opening the rest of a batch.

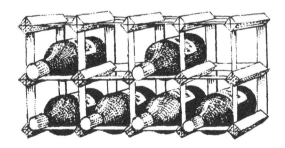

SPARKLING WINES

If you want bubbly, be it gooseberry 'Champagne' or sparkling apple, there is one more process to be undertaken before bottling. This will add a little to the total winemaking time, but it is well worth the effort. What you have to do is arrange for the very last part of the fermentation to happen in the bottle. Because the finished wine has bubbles of carbon dioxide in it, it will need to be in a specially strengthened bottle, with a wired-down cork.

There are two main methods for sparkling wines – one uses sugar in the bottles and the other relies on the accurate use of a hydrometer. For the sugar method, choose a dry wine and leave it to work itself out (the specific gravity will be well under 1.000 if you use a hydrometer, see page 39). Add ½ teaspoon of sugar to each Champagne bottle and pour in the wine. Now put in the special corks, according to the instructions and, using a pair of pliers, tighten the wires to stop the corks flying out. Lay down the bottles for at least a month and the sugar will be converted into extra alcohol and bubbles of carbon dioxide. Some of the old recipes use a couple of raisins in each bottle instead of sugar.

For the other method, check the specific gravity of the wine with a hydrometer and when it has reached *1.000 exactly*, rack off, bottle and cork as above. There is still enough sugar in the must for that extra bit of fermentation in the bottle. Just store the bottles for a month or two at the right temperature and leave the rest to happen. This is not the true 'méthode champenoise', but is a much easier method to use at home. Unless you are very experienced, DO NOT TRY TO ADD SPARKLE TO A VERY SWEET WINE. Exploding bottles and flying corks can be very dangerous.

·7·
HELPFUL HINTS

Most winemakers make batch upon batch of country wines without encountering any problems, but sometimes you may find that as you taste your wine at each stage, it is not turning out quite as you expected.

The first question is to decide whether it really is a problem at all. If your wine has a slight sediment, for example, it will not alter the taste, and it will be in the company of the most expensive and sought-after French wines and vintage ports! Decant it carefully and enjoy it.

On other occasions, there may be something you can do to put things right, or you can use the wine for blending to make something really individual and special. At the worst, you can use the wine for cooking and you will have learnt a valuable lesson for your next batch of wine.

ELDERFLOWER ICE CUBES *Flowers, of course, have wonderful perfumes and for this reason they are sometimes used to make ice cubes to add bouquet to a fruit wine. Elderflowers are particularly suitable. Pour a little boiling water (not too much – this needs to be concentrated) on to the flowers, then pour the perfumed water into ice cube trays. When frozen, seal them well in polythene bags and store them in the freezer. They can be dropped into wine musts whenever a flower bouquet is desired.*

COMMON PROBLEMS

Here is a quick A to Z of common problems, some of which you may be unlucky enough to encounter in your winemaking, and some simple solutions.

Acid Flavour   Perhaps the ingredients you used contained too much acid, so be more careful next time. Keep this wine for blending with a low-acid one.

Bland Wine   A bland wine is sometimes lacking in acid or tannin, which gives 'bite' to the wine. You can add a teaspoonful of lemon juice or strong black tea, cooled and strained, to the fermenting wine and leave it to work itself out.

If you decide to blend the finished wine, mix it with a wine which is high in acid, such as rhubarb.

Poor Bouquet   This may be due to poor ingredients or lack of acid. You can add flower bouquets to white wines by stirring some elderflower or rose petals into the fermentation bucket, or you can add some elderflower ice cubes (see opposite).

Bubbly Wine   Unless you intended making a sparkling wine, a tingling sensation on the tongue means the wine is still fermenting. Seal the demijohn with an airlock and leave it in a warm place until it has worked itself out.

Cloudy Wine   If your wine is cloudy and slow to clear, it could just be that you are too impatient; leave it a little longer to finish fermenting. If the wine has finished fermenting, siphon it into a clean demijohn, seal with a rubber bung and leave it in peace for a while.

If the cloudiness persists, there is an easy way to clear it.

Bake an eggshell or two in a slow oven (today you could microwave it on low) until it is dry and crumbles easily. Put 1 teaspoonful of crumbled eggshell into 1 gallon (4.5 l) of wine and leave it for a few weeks – the effect is quite startling. Siphon off the wine very carefully.

If the wine is already bottled, simply add a good pinch of crumbled eggshell to each bottle and wait for the magic results.

There are other clearing agents which you can find in home-brew shops, but their effect will be similar to this simple and natural old-fashioned remedy and they may add unwanted chemicals to your wine. It is up to you whether you choose to try them and read the label carefully! The main clearing or fining agents are Bentonite, made from clay, and gelatin and isinglass, made from fish and bones. You mix these with a little of the wine in a sterile jar, leave for 24 hours, then pour the liquid back into the demijohn and leave the wine to settle for at least a week before siphoning off into a clean demijohn.

Sometimes a haze in a wine can be caused by pectin or starch in the main ingredients. The wine can be treated to clear the haze: pectinase is a pectin-destroying enzyme and amylase is a starch-destroying enzyme. They are available in powder or liquid form from home-brew shops.

Over-sweet Wine   If your fermenting wine tastes too sweet, it may be that it has not worked itself out, even though fermentation appears to have finished. This is called a 'stuck fermentation', which means that the yeast has stopped growing and multiplying. The most common cause of this is temperature, so if you suspect that the demijohn has been kept in too warm or too cold a place, move it to a more appropriate spot.

Another cause of a stuck fermentation is that there was insufficient acid or nutrient for the yeast to grow, so check your list of ingredients (you did write them down on a label, didn't you?) and if one of these essentials seems to be lacking, stir in a teaspoon of lemon juice or ½ teaspoon of yeast nutrient. You can do this as you rack the wine from one jar to another – indeed sometimes the act of racking itself will restart a fermentation by aerating the wine.

If all else fails, buy a sachet of special yeast 'for stuck fermentations'. Siphon off a little of the must into a clean bottle and start the yeast working in this with a little warm water. Then add the yeast to the demijohn, cross your fingers and hope the yeast goes on growing.

Over-dry Wine Some years the natural sugars in the fruit etc. are not as high as others and you may find some of your wines a little dry. I have found that it is simple to add a *very* small amount of sugar solution to taste to correct this, but don't overdo it! You may start off a secondary fermentation.

Vinegar Taste In the early stages, if the vinegar taste is only faint, you may be able to rescue the wine by adding a crushed Campden tablet to the must. Leave it for 24 hours then introduce some new yeast.

At a later stage, just accept that your wine has been infected by the vinegar bacteria and make sure you are more careful next time to sterilise everything and to keep the wine well covered.

You can always use the wine vinegar in cooking or pickling, but do not try to blend it with another wine – you will just turn the lot into vinegar.

Yeasty or Musty Flavour The wine is probably too young and has not finished fermenting. Siphon into a clean demijohn, seal with an airlock and leave to ferment in a warm place until it has worked itself out.

With a few country wines, this may mean that you have left the wine on the sediment for too long. Blend the wine with one with a more powerful flavour or use it for cooking. Next time, remember to siphon off that particular wine sooner than before.

USING A HYDROMETER

A hydrometer is an instrument which tells you the specific gravity of your wine. This is the mass of the liquid compared with water, which has an SG of 1.000. To a new winemaker, it all sounds very technical and complicated, but in fact using a hydrometer is simply a way of finding out how much sugar there is in your wine, and therefore how much alcohol it does or will contain.

The winemakers we have met in making the *Fruity Passions* television series have fallen into two schools of thought on hydrometers. Either they have never seen such a thing, let alone used one, and their wine does not suffer in the least, or they claim that it is well nigh impossible to make consistently good wine without one. The choice is yours.

The hydrometer is a calibrated glass or plastic instrument which looks a bit like a thermometer, except that it does not contain mercury or coloured alcohol. It is designed to float upright in a special tube, like a measuring cylinder, which you fill with must or wine. You make a reading at the point at which the hydrometer breaks the surface of the wine. If the liquid is dense and full of sugar, the hydrometer will be buoyant and float high, but if there is very little sugar, the hydrometer will sink low.

The first stage at which you can test the SG of your wine is when you have strained the fermenting liquid into the demijohn. By referring to the tables which come with the hydrometer, you can calculate the potential alcohol level of your finished wine, which is determined by the amount of sugar in the must. Therefore if you want a predetermined alcoholic content, you can test and adjust the SG of your must by either diluting it with water or adding sugar syrup.

To take a reading, pour some of the must into the hydrometer float jar until it is nearly full. The must should be between 50°F (10°C) and 70°F (21°C) or you will get an inaccurate reading. Lower the hydrometer into the liquid with the heavy end at the bottom. Shake the hydrometer to dislodge any air bubbles, then leave it to settle. When it stops bobbing up and down, read the numbers on the hydrometer at the exact point where it breaks the surface of the liquid.

As the wine ferments, the specific gravity will drop. If you think that fermentation is not complete, even though carbon dioxide is no longer being released, you can check whether you have a stuck fermentation by testing with a hydrometer to be sure whether the sugar has been used up. If the wine has not worked itself out, you can try the remedies listed under 'Over-sweet Wine' above.

·8·
BLENDING WINES

There are two methods of blending, either by mixing the ingredients at fermentation time when, unless you are very experienced, it is impossible to judge what the final outcome will be, or by actually tasting then blending the finished wines.

I much prefer the latter method and not just because I have many happy warm memories of cold wet wintery nights tasting, blending and enjoying the exhilarating fun of creating a unique wine.

Your wines will vary from season to season, county to county, in fact from hedgerow to hedgerow, and individual palates vary in sharpness. Always remember that the wines you most enjoy are the wines you will most enjoy making, so don't worry if your taste varies from that of other winemakers and so-called experts; it's your wine, your choice. You have the ability to change the character of your wine after fermentation has ceased if you feel that you can improve the flavour.

Never attempt to blend your wine before it has become really stable, as dormant yeast cells can easily restart a ferment by the addition of a sweeter wine, or simply by the addition of a sugar syrup if you are trying to achieve a sweet wine finish.

It will take you a little time to learn the art of blending, but the main thing to remember is, don't try to improve a poor wine by blending with a really good one. You will only end up with a mediocre example.

Start by blending small quantities and do not be afraid to use combinations of several rather than just two wines. But keep the types of wine you blend as simple as possible: fruit with flowers, root with root or bower (leaf and sap). It is advisable to leave the blended wine in a demijohn for a day or two before bottling.

Of course even when you have arrived at what you think is a rich red or a fine dry or a wonderful fruity blend, you have to remember that time will have a hand in the finished result. In other words, most wines still need time to mature after blending.

Have fun, don't try too many at one time – your taste buds may become a little blurred – and don't ask too many friends or family to help; it has to be your choice. You will never please everyone but you will enjoy trying.

·9·

SPRING RECIPES

— *DANDELIONS* —

Dandelion wine has always been one of my favourites; partly because of my palate and partly because of all the happy memories evoked by this delicious wine. It epitomises for me the joy of all winemaking.

The whole family was involved in picking the golden flower heads. Usually we made a morning of it, followed by a super picnic with home-made pork pies, hard-boiled eggs and crusty home-made breads accompanied by a glass of last year's (or an even older) dandelion wine.

The tradition seems to be that you should pick the dandelions on or near St George's Day, but we did not adhere to this. If the spring was very wet and we didn't get a good first crop of flowers, or if we were too busy ploughing and sowing, we would wait for the second flush of dandelions in the summer. They probably wouldn't be as lush as the first flowers and the wine would taste different, but still good.

Oh! how I loved those days. Yet one of my clearest and earliest memories is of hopping from one foot to another, putting off the moment when my gunged-up fingers, yellow with pollen, had to negotiate my knicker elastic! Would my mother be cross if my fingers stained them yellow? Or even more cross if I left it too late? I am not sure whether the fact that dandelions are diuretic had anything to do with it – they are known as pee-the-beds (or *pissenlits* in France) and the wine is known to be good for flushing out the kidneys.

Whatever the trials of picking the petals I am certain that my love of home-made wine stems (pardon the pun) from those early golden days.

Dandelion Wine

6 pints (3.4 l) dandelion flowers
Finely peeled rind and juice of 1
   orange
Finely peeled rind and juice of 1
   lemon

8 pints (4.5 l) water
3 lb (1.5 kg) sugar
4 fl oz (120 ml) strong black tea,
   cooled and strained
1/4 oz (10 g) wine yeast

Taking care to discard all the green parts, I pick the dandelion heads straight into a muslin bag or an old pillow case: the original boil-in-the-bag. Add the orange and lemon rind to the dandelion heads, secure the top of the bag and place in a large saucepan with the water. Bring to the boil and simmer for 20 minutes. Remove the bag, squeezing it to remove all the liquid, and dissolve the sugar in the liquid. Pour it into a fermentation bucket and add the orange and lemon juice and the tea. Start the yeast, then add it to the cooled must. Cover and leave to work for 3 to 5 days, stirring daily.

Siphon into a demijohn, seal with an airlock and leave for about 2 to 3 months to work itself out.

When fermentation has quite finished, siphon into storage jars or bottles. This great family favourite is ready for drinking with the Christmas turkey, but will improve with keeping – the longer the better.

Make sure no agricultural sprays have been used on the dandelions before you pick them.

Dandelion Beer

I remember drinking this straight from the bottles when no-one was about. It surely is one of the finest thirst quenchers and not very alcoholic. It is a wonderful way to use up all the young dandelion plants in the spring and much better for the family than some of the modern cordials. My mother used to recommend it to all the young men in the village who suffered from acne – there was always a steady stream for her cure. Father was never convinced of the healing power of this potion – he felt that his seven daughters were much more likely to be the attraction – cynic! I still think it's worth a try and it's so easy to make.

8 oz (225 g) young dandelion
    plants
8 pints (4.5 l) water
½ oz (15 g) root ginger, bruised
Finely peeled rind and juice of
    1 lemon

1 lb (450 g) demerara sugar
1 oz (25 g) cream of tartar
¼ oz (10 g) brewers' yeast

Dig up the complete young plants in the spring, wash them well and remove the fibrous roots, leaving the main tap root. Place in a large saucepan with the water, bruised ginger and finely peeled lemon rind, bring to the boil and simmer for 10 minutes. Strain and pour on to the sugar and cream of tartar in a fermentation bucket. Stir until the sugar has dissolved. Start the yeast, then add it to the lukewarm must with the lemon juice. Cover and leave in a warm room for 3 days.

Strain into strong, screw-top bottles. This delicious brew can be drunk in about a week when it has cleared.

— OTHER FLOWERS —

Wallflower Wine

In Shropshire we call this Gillieflower Wine. The first time I attempted this sweet-smelling wine I was not confident about the outcome – Doubting Thomas that I was. The end result was a delightful light table wine, not over scented as I had expected, and ready to drink before the year was out.

½ pint (300 ml) wallflower
*   petals*
1 lb (450 g) sultanas, washed
*   and chopped*
2½ lb (1.25 kg) sugar

Juice of 2 lemons
8 pints (4.5 l) water
¼ oz (10 g) wine yeast

Pick the petals dry, preferably with the sun on them, and use them immediately. Place the petals, sultanas, sugar and lemon juice in a fermentation bucket and pour on the boiling water. Stir well and allow to cool. Start the yeast, before adding it to the bucket. Cover and leave for 7 days, stirring daily.

    Strain into a demijohn, seal with an airlock and leave to ferment for about 2 to 3 months until it has worked itself out.

    When the wine is clear, siphon into storage jars or bottles.

Broom or Gorse Wine

This recipe is really for gorse. My mother used to send us out picking the flowers but oh! how I hated those needle-sharp spikes! I changed to broom some years ago and any deterioration in the flavour was more than compensated for by the ease of gathering. However, if you have the hide of a rhinoceros and happier memories than me about the lowly gorse, do use it.

8 pints (4.5 l) water
3 lb (1.5 kg) sugar
Finely peeled rind and juice of 2
*   lemons*
Finely peeled rind and juice of 1
*   orange*

4 pints (2.25 l) broom or gorse
*   flowers*
¼ oz (10 g) wine yeast

Boil the water in a large saucepan and add the sugar and lemon and orange rind and juice. Stir until the sugar has completely dissolved. Pour on to the flowers in a fermentation bucket and mash together. Start the yeast, then add it to the cooled must. Leave for 3 to 4 days, mashing the flowers twice daily.

Strain into a demijohn and seal with an airlock. Allow to ferment for about 2 to 3 months until it has worked itself out.

When the wine is clear and bright, siphon it into bottles. This wine is best kept for 6 to 12 months before drinking.

— HEDGEROWS —

If you avoid busy roads and stray off the beaten track, there are still ample harvests to be picked from our country hedgerows, but do remember to leave some young growth and flowers for the plants themselves as they are one of our richest inheritances and we must take great care of them and encourage new growth.

Bramble Tip Wine

This is a true hedgerow wine. Gather the top 2 or 3 in (5 or 7 cm) of the bramble (blackberry bush) tips in the spring when they have more flavour.

4 pints (2.25 l) bramble tips   *¼ oz (10 g) wine yeast*
4 pints (2.25 l) water   *¼ teaspoon yeast nutrient*
1½ lb (750 g) sugar

Place the bramble tips in a large saucepan and cover with cold water. Bring to the boil and simmer for 30 minutes. Strain on to the sugar in a fermentation bucket and stir until the sugar has dissolved. Start the yeast by mixing it with the yeast nutrient and a little of the must, then add it to the cooled must. Pour into a demijohn and seal with an airlock. Allow to ferment until it has worked itself out.

Siphon into bottles or storage jars. This wine is best kept for at least a year before drinking.

I have also made Bramble Tip Wine by simmering the bramble tips for 15 minutes then leaving them to stand overnight. Strain them on to the sugar, add a little cold black tea or grape tannin, ½ teaspoon of citric acid, the yeast and pour into a demijohn. Seal with an airlock and allow to work itself out.

— LEAVES AND HERBS —

Wigley Oak Leaf Wine

I have already mentioned the effect Mrs Wigley's wine had on many of the villagers and friends who have tasted it. It is a pleasant enough wine but do be careful not to over-indulge as its reputation for 'leg-buckling' is renowned. I usually serve it as an aperitif topped up with cold lemonade. Like the mighty oak it takes quite a while to mature – at least 2 years – after which time it will become light and dry.

8 pints (4.5 l) young oak leaves
8 oz (225 g) sultanas, washed
* and chopped*
Juice of 2 lemons
¼ teaspoon pure malt extract

2 lb (1 kg) granulated sugar
8 pints (4.5 l) water
¼ oz (10 g) wine yeast

Cut all stems from the young oak leaves, rinse them well and gently press into a calibrated jug or bucket to measure. Place into your fermentation bucket with the rinsed and chopped sultanas, lemon juice and pure malt extract. Dissolve the sugar in 1 pint (600 ml) of boiled water and allow to cool. Pour on to the oak leaves and top up with 7 pints (3.9 l) of cold water. Start the yeast, then add it to the fermentation bucket and stir well. Cover tightly and let it stand for at least 10 days, stirring daily.

Siphon off into a demijohn, top up to the neck with cooled boiled water, seal with an airlock and leave to ferment for 5 to 6 weeks.

Let it be still for a further 2 to 3 weeks before siphoning off into a clean jar. Top up to the neck with some you have already made (or cooled boiled water if you haven't any). It will take a year to clear and another year to mature.

Agrimony Wine

This lovely plant with its slender yellow flower spikes is less common in the herb garden than the hedge banks and on waste ground.

A good bunch of agrimony leaves   *2 lemons, sliced*
8 pints (4.5 l) water   *2 oranges, sliced*
3 lb (1.5 kg) sugar   *¼ oz (10 g) wine yeast*

Gently boil the agrimony in the water for about 40 minutes. Pour on to the sugar and sliced fruit and stir well. Start the yeast, then add it to the cooled must. Cover and leave for 3 days.

Strain into a demijohn, seal with an airlock and leave to work itself out.

Siphon into bottles. It will be ready to use after a few months.

Tansy Wine

This wine is slightly gingery in flavour and makes a good warming punch with orange juice and honey.

8 pints (4.5 l) water   *4 fl oz (120 ml) strong black tea,*
A large handful of tansy leaves   *cooled and strained*
Juice of 2 lemons   *¼ oz (10 g) wine yeast*
3 lb (1.5 kg) sugar

Pour the boiling water over all the ingredients, except the yeast, in a fermentation bucket. Stir well and allow to cool until lukewarm. Start the yeast, then add it to the bucket. Cover and leave to ferment for 3 days.

Strain into a demijohn, seal with an airlock and leave to work itself out.

Siphon into bottles. This wine does not need much keeping.

Mrs Bray's Fennel Wine

'It is much used in drink to make people more lean that are too fat.'
Culpeper. This must be one of the oldest slimming recipes known.
It uses the feathery fennel herb, not root fennel.

1 bunch of fresh fennel
5 pints (2.75 l) water
3½ lb (1.5 kg) sugar — 4 lb
(1.75 kg) if you like it sweet
1 oz (25 g) dried fennel
½ pint (300 ml) strong black
tea, cooled and strained

½ pint (300 ml) redcurrant
juice
½ pint (300 ml) grape juice
Juice of 2 lemons
1 teaspoon citric acid
1 slice toast
1–2 teaspoons active dried yeast

Put the fresh fennel in a fermentation bucket and pour on the
boiling water. Leave for 1 hour and then strain on to the sugar.
When cool, add the rest of the ingredients, except the toast and
yeast, and stir until dissolved, then float a piece of toast on the top
sprinkled with the dried yeast. Keep in a warm place for 2 to 3
days, stirring occasionally.

Strain into a demijohn, seal with an airlock and leave until
fermentation has stopped and the wine begins to clear.

Siphon off for the first time into a clean demijohn and seal with a
rubber bung. Leave for about 3 to 4 months until completely clear.

Siphon into bottles.

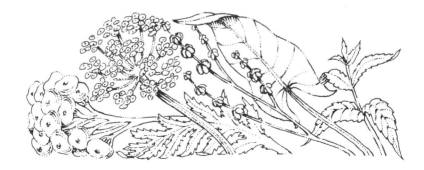

Parsley Wine

This wine has been used medicinally by country folk to keep rheumatism at bay.

1 lb (450 g) parsley
8 pints (4.5 l) water
2 lb (1 kg) honey
Finely peeled rind and juice of
    2 oranges

Finely peeled rind and juice of
    2 lemons
¼ oz (10 g) wine yeast

Place the washed parsley (I use the stems an' all) in a fermentation bucket, pour on the boiling water and leave to infuse for 24 hours.

Strain on to the honey and orange and lemon rind and juice in a fermentation bucket. Start the yeast, then add it to the bucket. Cover and leave to ferment for 4 to 5 days.

Strain into a demijohn, seal with an airlock and leave to work itself out.

Siphon into bottles. This wine needs no keeping. Do try it in a vegetable casserole – delicious.

— NETTLES —

I make no apologies for including nettles in my recipes even though, like the nettle soup I have served in my restaurant, they have mixed appeal. The wine has a clean herby flavour and the tea, with the rich chlorophyll from the young nettle tips, is very good for the complexion and will save you pounds on preparatory lotions. The beer is quick and easy to make. 'Grasp the nettle' and have a go!

Nettle Wine

Please make sure you wash the freshly picked nettles, and only use the very topmost young shoots. The less intrepid who believe they will get stung can wear gloves – but don't cheat by using the 'dead nettle', which hasn't the same flavour.

4 pints (2.25 l) nettle tips
12 oz (350 g) sultanas, washed and chopped
2 lb (1 kg) granulated sugar
4 fl oz (120 ml) strong black tea, cooled and strained
Juice of 2 lemons

8 pints (4.5 l) boiling water
¼ oz (10 g) wine yeast
¼ teaspoon yeast extract or yeast nutrient
4 fl oz (120 ml) warm water
1 teaspoon sugar

Place nettle tips, sultanas, sugar, tea and lemon juice in a fermentation bucket, pour on the boiling water and stir well. Mix the yeast and yeast nutrient with the warm water and sugar. Leave until it begins to bubble, then stir it into the bucket. Cover and leave for 7 to 10 days, stirring daily.

Strain the wine into a demijohn, top up with cooled boiled water, seal with an airlock and leave for 4 to 5 weeks until it has worked itself out.

Let it rest for about another week, then siphon into another jar, top up again and bung tightly. Keep in a cool place for about 6 months when it should be ready to bottle.

Nettle Tea

What better way to start the day than with this cleansing drink with its earthy bouquet?

Just pour boiling water over 2 or 3 nettle tips in your breakfast cup and flavour with honey or lemon or both.

Nettle Beer

This is a refreshing spring or early summer drink, not a wine, and it is ready for drinking in about a week. Brimming tumblers are served with a slice of lemon, cucumber, a sprig or two of young mint and some ice. Your friends will be surprised and delighted at the unusual flavour and your smile of satisfaction will be enhanced by knowing you have not been stung in your pocket.

1 lb (450 g) nettle tips
Finely peeled rind and juice of 1
*   lemon*
4 pints (2.25 l) water

8 oz (225 g) demerara sugar
½ oz (15 g) cream of tartar
¼ oz (10 g) brewers' yeast

Place the nettle tips, finely peeled lemon rind and water in a large saucepan. Bring to the boil and simmer for 30 minutes. Strain on to the sugar and cream of tartar in a fermentation bucket and stir well. Start the yeast, then add it to the cooled must with the lemon juice. Cover and leave in a warm room for about 3 days.

Strain into strong bottles – cider flagons will do – but do not screw up too tightly as the beer is slightly effervescent. Nettle beer does not have a long life but you should really give it a week or two to settle before drinking.

It makes a jolly good stock for a rich vegetable casserole – just gives that extra something.

— RHUBARB —

The best rhubarb wine is made from Champagne rhubarb – about the sweetest one you can grow – but don't worry if your crowns are not jewelled: ordinary rhubarb makes a passable wine. Just make sure you pick it whilst it is still young, pink and fresh. Don't forget that the leaves and the green parts of the stalk are poisonous.

Gerry Fowles' Rhubarb Wine

I learned this recipe from Gerry Fowles, Professor of Chemistry at Reading University. Freezing the rhubarb softens it and makes it possible to squeeze out the juice.

2 lb (1 kg) rhubarb, previously frozen
1 lb (450 g) sultanas, washed and chopped
5½ pint (3.3 l) water

1 lb 6 oz (625 g) sugar
¼ teaspoon yeast nutrient
1 tablet pectolitic enzyme
¼ oz (10 g) wine yeast

Squeeze the rhubarb through a muslin bag to collect the juice. Soak the sultanas in the water to plump them up, then put them in a fermentation bucket. Add the rhubarb juice and the sugar. Stir well. Add the yeast nutrient and pectolitic enzyme. Start the yeast and add it to the bucket, then stir well. Cover with a lid and leave in a warm place for 3 to 4 days, stirring daily.

Siphon into a demijohn, seal with an airlock and leave for about 2 to 3 months to work itself out.

When fermentation has finished, siphon into a clean demijohn, seal with a rubber bung and leave to mature.

Bottle up, if you wish, when the wine has completely cleared.

Rhubarb Wine Pie

Why not try a Rhubarb Wine Pie with some of the pulp? Use half the pulp and mix in a tablespoonful of ginger marmalade. Cover with shortcrust pastry and bake in a moderate oven at 350°F (180°C), gas mark 4 for 25 to 30 minutes. Hey presto! Rhubarb Wine Pie.

·10·
SUMMER RECIPES

— *ELDERFLOWERS* —

Why, oh why are we not making more use of one of mother nature's most wonderful gifts! It is summer time and hedgerows everywhere are dressed over all in a wonderful white array – thousands and thousands of elderflower heads. Forgive me if I seem to be waxing lyrical over these lovely creamy white blossoms but my love affair with the elderflower goes back a long way. One of nature's most versatile gifts, it has, in my opinion, a magical quality and so very many uses – in wines, cordials, desserts, preserves, garnishes and even cosmetics to name but a few – and all for the picking. I hardly know where to begin. Why not let us literally add a little sparkle to life by starting with Elderflower Champagne!

Elderflower Champagne

One of the most successful parties I have ever given was, I am sure, due almost entirely to this easy-to-make, sparkling elixir. Let me tell the story.

To raise money for tree planting round the village my friend, Sarah, and I hit on the idea of a baroque musical evening – music in the church followed by supper and drinks at the farm – Sarah to arrange the music and musicians and I the food and wine.

Working on a very tight budget didn't leave me anything for conventional wine and I worried for days and nights about just what to do. There was only one solution and that was to make gallons of Elderflower Champagne.

What a night it turned out to be – mid-summer, warm, balmy, the still air full of music, love and laughter, everyone spilling out into the garden thirsting for more wine with their supper. I, trying not to reveal its humble origin, was kept very busy filling up their glasses. They gradually became more and more 'at one' with themselves and each other, happily unaware of the low alcohol content of the wine, some of which was less than ten days old.

Was it the tiny wild flower bouquets picked by Sarah's little daughter, the music, the food, the balmy night, the company or was it the Champagne that produced the spirit of happiness at that mid-summer soirée? Perhaps a little of each. Whatever, people still talk of it with pure pleasure. Never again will I be ashamed to serve up my humble country elderflower with its magical, intoxicating qualities.

Try it. I made 15 gallons (68 l) for the cost of the sugar and lemons and little else, more than enough for 130 people – hardly expensive entertaining!

5–6 elderflower heads	*2 tablespoons cider vinegar*, or
2 lemons, sliced	*½ oz (15 g) citric acid*
8 pints (4.5 l) boiled water	
1½ lb (750 g) sugar	

Put the elderflower heads and sliced lemons in a fermentation bucket and pour on the water. Leave to soak for 24–36 hours. Strain through a cloth or fine sieve and add the sugar and the vinegar or citric acid. Stir well until the sugar is completely dissolved and either pour into Champagne bottles (in which case you'll need to use wired corks – a rather complex procedure) or screw-top bottles. If you use the latter *don't* screw up the tops very tightly for about 7–14 days. This is because the Champagne continues to work itself out in the bottles.

This delicious nose-tickling drink isn't honestly a Champagne and doesn't keep much longer than 3 months, but you can have such fun with it!

Elderflower Fritters

These are simplicity itself to make and provide a wholesome and delightful feast for young and old alike. Why not surprise your friends with this green cuisine, especially when eating out of doors? I can assure you they will find them scrumptious.

12 elderflower heads	*Vegetable or sunflower oil for*
8 oz (225 g) plain flour	*deep frying*
2 eggs	*Caster sugar for dusting*
½ pint (300 ml) milk	

Pick the whole flower heads – not from the roadside because we do not want lead-laden flowers. Wash them and shake off excess moisture. Mix the flour, eggs and milk to a batter. Dust the flower heads with plain flour and, holding by the stem, dip them into the batter. Deep fry in vegetable or sunflower oil for about 1 minute or until golden and crispy. Drain on some kitchen paper and dust with caster sugar.

The fritters are equally delicious hot or cold. I serve them as a dessert, adding a few chopped almonds plus a good dollop of whipped cream and, for sheer extravagance, dribble over a little pure raspberry or strawberry syrup.

— GROUND ELDER —

The story of how I heard about this wine epitomises many of the beliefs I hold. God, in his infinite wisdom, has decreed that mother nature, occasionally with a little help from us, will provide. What a lovely story this is. I am blessed with some dear friends whose spiritual and loving support help me much more than they can ever imagine. They are the Sisters of the St Denys Convent, a Church of England community in Warminster. Sister Lucy, now in her 90s, has tended the garden for more years than she cares to remember and come rain, come shine, has never been known to waste anything that the Lord provides. We are great friends and both being Shropshire lassies is an added bond. But now to the wine . . .

Sister Carol's Ground Elder Flower Wine

The story goes, according to Sister Carol who helps make the country wines purely for the occasional celebration day, that some years ago Sister Lucy had taken over a piece of ground rather well endowed with the curse of all gardeners – ground elder. The young man put to the task of clearing the patch, rotovated it in and thereby doubled the growth! Walking in disgust through this carpet of flowering weeds Sister Lucy became aware that the bees were having a field day. She stood reflecting that out of an apparently useless situation can come some good – the honey would be wonderful and, as she puts it, the bees told her that the ground elder flowers could be harvested for Sister Carol to turn into wine. Sister Carol laughingly tells me how they made the wine, then wrote to the magazine, *Gardeners' World*, to record this wonder and were rewarded with a £1 postal order! The wine was as good as that year's elderflower from the trees.

I have to admit I never tried it, thankfully managing to keep the dreaded weed under control, but the moral of the story remains ever with me.

*1 pint (600 ml) ground elder
  flower heads
12 oz (350 g) pure honey
8 pints (4.5 l) water
Juice of 2 lemons*

*4 fl oz (120 ml) strong black tea,
  cooled and strained
½ teaspoon yeast nutrient
¼ oz (10 g) wine yeast*

Remove the flowers from the stems, wash them well and place them in a fermentation bucket. Heat the honey in about 1 pint (600 ml) of the water until it has dissolved. Allow to cool. Pour on to the flower heads with the lemon juice, cold tea, yeast nutrient and the remainder of the water. Start the yeast, then add it to the bucket. Stir well, cover and leave in a warm place for 10 days, stirring twice daily.

Strain the liquid into a fermentation jar, top up to the neck with cooled boiled water, seal with an airlock and leave working away until fermentation has ceased.

Siphon off into another clean jar, leaving all the sediment behind. Top up with elderflower cordial or cooled boiled water. Close tightly with a rubber bung and leave for about 6 months to clear and mature. It is then ready for bottling. However, for a worthwhile weed wine wait for the winter weather before drinking!

— HONEYSUCKLE —

I've never been able to bring myself to make this wine. I've collected the flowers on many occasions but they have ended up in vases scenting the whole house, or in my face creams. Using an infusion of the flower heads in refined goose fat as a cleanser and softener is lovely. I've even heard it said that its greatest property is as an aphrodisiac.

Please remember that the berries of the honeysuckle are poisonous.

Mrs Smith's Honeysuckle Wine

Here is a recipe given to me by a dear old lady in the village who had the reputation for curing asthma and freckles with her honeysuckle wine. I have done a little up-dating of the original recipe.

2 pints (1.2 l) honeysuckle
   flowers
2½ lb (1.25 kg) sugar
1 lb (450 g) sultanas, washed
   and chopped
2 teaspoons citric acid

2 fl oz (50 ml) strong black tea,
   cooled and strained
6 pints (3.4 l) water
¼ oz (10 g) wine yeast

Use only the flower heads and put them in a fermentation bucket with the sugar, sultanas, citric acid and cold tea. Add the boiling water and stir until the sugar has dissolved. Start the yeast, then add it to the cooled must. Cover and leave for 4 to 5 days, stirring daily.

Strain into a demijohn, top up to the neck with water and seal with an airlock. Leave to ferment for about 3 months when it will be ready for bottling.

The wine will be medium sweet and will improve with keeping.

— OTHER FLOWERS —

Rose Petal Wine

This delightful fragrant wine has many uses apart from drinking! I use it to cook my fish, especially fresh trout. Decorate your wine dish with a few fresh rose petals; it makes a pleasant and surprising change from parsley and dill.

Use freshly picked fragrant petals and do ensure that they have not been sprayed with pesticide or herbicide.

4 pints (2.25 l) rose petals	*Juice of 2 oranges*
8 pints (4.5 l) water	*3 lb (1.5 kg) sugar*
Juice of 2 lemons	*1/4–1/2 oz (10–15 g) wine yeast*

Place the petals in a fermentation bucket, cover with boiling water and steep for 4 days, stirring from time to time.

Strain through a fine sieve into a demijohn. Add enough cooled boiled water to make up to 8 pints (4.5 l). Stir in the lemon and orange juice and sugar. Start the yeast, then add it to the must. Seal with an airlock and leave to work itself out.

Siphon into a clean demijohn, seal with a bung and leave for 7 to 8 months to mature before bottling. I haven't found it necessary to keep this wine much longer after bottling.

Rose Petal Sandwiches

On a summer's day why not make rose petal sandwiches to accompany last year's Rose Hip wine? – but please make sure you have not sprayed your roses beforehand.

I have updated my mother's recipe.

4 oz (100 g) butter	*8 thin slices freshly baked*
A good handful of red rose petals	*wholemeal bread*

Place the butter on a square of tin foil and completely cover with rose petals. Wrap up well to ensure the parcel is air-tight and place in the refrigerator overnight.

Using a saucer as a guide, cut the bread into circles. Spread with the fragrant petal butter and cover with a few fresh red petals, making sure they stick out at the edges of the bread. Cut into four and arrange attractively on your plates.

My sisters add caster sugar, but in my opinion these sandwiches don't need any additional flavour and they look so pretty.

Marigold Wine

3 lb (1.5 kg) sugar
8 pints (4.5 l) water
4 pints (2.25 l) marigold flower
*   heads*

Finely peeled rind and juice of
*   2 oranges*
Finely peeled rind and juice of
*   1 lemon*
¼ oz (10 g) wine yeast

Dissolve the sugar in the water in a large saucepan and bring to the boil. Pour on to the flower heads and the orange and lemon rind and juice in a fermentation bucket. Allow to cool. Start the yeast, then add it to the cooled must. Stir well, cover and leave to ferment for at least 7 days in a warm place.

Strain into a fermentation jar, seal with an airlock and leave in a warm place to work itself out.

When still, leave for a further 4 weeks before bottling off. The wine will be ready for drinking almost immediately. It is best served chilled and is lovely for picnics.

— RASPBERRIES —

Granny's Raspberry Wine

Granny's recipe, which is dated 1852, doesn't give any definite quantities, which is useful as it means you can make quite small amounts. The only problem is that you must use smaller container jars for fermenting – old cider flagons which hold 2 pints (1.2 l) are useful. Anyway, here is the recipe from her book.

Bruise the raspberries well. Strain through a fine jelly bag or sieve. Measure the juice and boil up an equal quantity of water. When cold, pour the water on to the fruit that you have strained. Stand for 24 hours and strain on to the juice already extracted. To every 1 pint (600 ml) of juice add 4 oz (100 g) sugar, then stir until it has dissolved. Pour into an earthenware stein or fermentation bucket. Spread a slice of toast with yeast and float it on top. Cover closely and leave to stand for 1 week.

Siphon off into a clean jar, seal with an airlock and allow to work itself out – it may take a month or two.

Siphon into bottles. It will be ready to drink almost immediately.

My Raspberry Wine

This is a light rosé type of wine which I very often use as a base for a cool summer cup or as a base for raspberry syrup which makes a lovely sweet salad dressing or is delicious trickled over ice-cream. If you can resist drinking it, it is best kept for at least a year.

3 lb (1.5 kg) raspberries   *2½ lb (1.25 kg) sugar*
8 pints (4.5 l) water   *¼ oz (10 g) wine yeast*

Gather the raspberries when ripe and dry, place them in a fermentation bucket and pour the boiling water over them. Cover well. The fly and wasp seem particularly partial to raspberries so be extra careful. Stir as often as you remember – at least twice a day for 4 to 5 days.

Strain into a clean demijohn, leaving enough room for the 'working', and add the sugar. Start the yeast, then add it to the demijohn and seal with an airlock. Save any surplus juice to top up with later – it keeps best bottled in the fridge. Leave to ferment until it has worked itself out.

When it has finished working, siphon off into a clean, sterile demijohn, top up to the neck with the saved juice, and bung tightly. Leave until you have time to rack off into bottles or decant into casks or jars.

Raspberry Gin

Some of you will know of Sloe Gin, made in October but not ready to drink for at least a year. Raspberry Gin, made in the summer, should be ready by Christmas. You will delight in the clear rosy glow both of the colour and the taste. I serve it after church with mince pies – it always goes down well.

2 lb (1 kg) ripe, warm	*1 pint (600 ml) gin*
raspberries — you won't all be	*2 pints (1.2 l) water*
able to gather them in the sun	*1 lb (450 g) sugar*
but get them as fresh as possible	

Place the cleaned fruit and gin in a large jar and leave to stand in a warm spot for 4 to 5 days, shaking the jar occasionally.

Bring the water to the boil in a large saucepan, add the sugar and boil gently for 10 to 15 minutes. Allow to cool and add to the fruit. Screw the jar up tightly and store in a dark cupboard for at least 3 months, occasionally turning the jar upside down. I have left it longer but found that it didn't improve the colour or the flavour.

Strain carefully through a fine jelly bag – the nylon ones are super these days. Bottle into small bottles. I usually fill some pretty little bottles to give as Christmas presents and my friends always enjoy them.

Raspberry Brandy

Raspberry Brandy can be made in exactly the same way as Raspberry Gin, using 1 lb (450 g) fruit to 1 pint (600 ml) brandy, and I add a good pinch of cinnamon and some cloves – this is a real 'cockles of your heart' warmer.

By the way, do use the fruit pulp from both the Raspberry Gin and the Raspberry Brandy as a base for a rich trifle or simply fill a Victoria sandwich cake and serve with fresh cream – blissfully scrumptious!

— OTHER SOFT FRUITS —

Redcurrant Wine

6 lb (2.75 kg) redcurrants   3 lb (1.5 kg) sugar
8 pints (4.5 l) water   ¼ oz (10 g) wine yeast

Place the redcurrants in a fermentation bucket and pour over the boiling water, mashing the fruit well to extract the juices. Cover and leave for 4 days, mashing and pressing the fruit daily.

Strain into a demijohn and stir in the sugar. Start the yeast and add it to the must. Seal with an airlock and leave to ferment for about 3 to 4 weeks at room temperature until it has worked itself out.

Siphon into a clean jar and top up, if necessary, with cooled boiled water; the jar must be full. Leave to mature for at least 10 months in dark bottles or jars.

Bottle and store for a further 6 months before drinking. I sometimes leave my Redcurrant Wine to finish fermenting in the bottles. It produces a light, delicate sparkling wine of high quality.

Redcurrant Rosé

3 lb (1.5 kg) redcurrants	*¼ oz (10 g) wine yeast*
3 lb (1.5 kg) sugar	*A little warm water*
8 pints (4.5 l) water	*1 teaspoon sugar*

De-stalk the redcurrants with a fork, wash them and crush them well in a fermentation bucket. Add the sugar and cold water and stir until the sugar has dissolved. Start the yeast with a little warm water and 1 teaspoon of sugar, then add it to the bucket. Leave to ferment on the pulp for 3 to 4 days, pressing down the fruit daily.

Strain through a fine sieve, pressing out all the juice into a demijohn, seal with an airlock and leave until the wine starts to clear.

Rack off into a clean demijohn and seal for at least a year, after which it will be ready to bottle.

This delightful wine may need a little sugar added to each bottle to suit your taste. Serve it well chilled or use it as a base for a refreshing fruit punch.

Blackcurrant Wine

3 lb (1.5 kg) blackcurrants	*8 pints (4.5 l) water*
3 lb (1.5 kg) sugar	*¼ oz (10 g) wine yeast*

Strip the currants, using a fork, and wash them well. Crush them into a fermentation bucket with the sugar. Pour on the boiling water, then allow to cool. Start the yeast, then add it to the must. Cover and leave to ferment for 4 to 5 days, stirring daily.

Strain off the liquid into a demijohn and seal with an airlock. Leave to work itself out.

Rack off into a clean demijohn when the wine starts to clear. Leave until fermentation has ceased.

Bottle off into dark bottles. Leave to mature in a cool, dark place. This wine does not take too long to mature – about 6 months.

— GOOSEBERRIES —

Mrs Bray's Gooseberry Wine

Dear Mrs Bray shared her favourite gooseberry wine recipe with me – what an absolute joy to meet someone who still makes country wines the original way – with no additives. She makes over 30 gallons (136 l) a year. I did not get to taste them all, but those I did sample were wonderful, proving yet again that the simple old methods remain the best.

4 lb (1.75 kg) ripe green gooseberries
8 pints (4.5 l) water
3 lb (1.5 kg) sugar

1 slice toast
¼ oz (10 g) granular wine yeast

Top and tail the berries, put them in a fermentation bucket and pour over the boiling water. When softened and cool enough, mash them with your hands. Cover and leave for 48 hours, stirring frequently.

Strain through a butter muslin on to the sugar and stir well until dissolved. Float a piece of toast on the top and sprinkle on the yeast. Leave to ferment for 3 to 4 days.

Strain into a demijohn and seal with an airlock. Leave to ferment to a finish before siphoning off into a storage jar.

Leave for another month before bottling. This is best drunk when the gooseberry bushes are in bloom the next year.

Gooseberry Champagne

My love of this light sparkling wine is well known to all my family and friends who have had it served up on many different occasions and in all kinds of guises: as a breakfast time special with orange juice; in stews and casseroles – my dear friend, Keith Floyd, loved it with rabbit; in puddings; in party punches; and as a sophisticated dinner drink it has few equals.

In the eighteenth century this was often sold as real Champagne, even by the French themselves, so it must have been good. Today this honest wine is well worth making as you can have so much fun with it.

By the way, I have a theory about the origin of the 'babies under a gooseberry bush' tale. These ugly little hairy berries seem to stay in touch with the mother bush. In other words you may well find that each flowering season the wine in your bottles will become slightly more effervescent – as if mother nature is calling her own – it's like the stirring of emotions at our children's birthday time. You don't believe me – well wait and see!

I have made this wine without the addition of any yeast, but a special Champagne yeast is available at most shops stocking winemaking equipment.

6 lb (2.75 kg) unripe green   *3 lb (1.5 kg) sugar*
  gooseberries   *¼ oz (10 g) Champagne yeast*
8 pints (4.5 l) water

Top and tail the berries and place them in a fermentation bucket. Pour over 4 pints (2.25 l) of boiling water. Stir well to squash the berries. When sufficiently cooled, use your hands to squeeze out even more juice. The fruit must be all broken but don't crush the bitter seeds. Cover well and leave for 24 hours.

Now you need to add the sugar. In order to ensure it dissolves properly, I find it is best to strain the fruit through a wire sieve and stir the sugar into the juice until it has dissolved. Then tip the sieved fruit back into the fermentation bucket and add the rest of the cold water. Squash the berries again, cover well and leave for 24 hours.

Strain through a wire sieve. Pour a little more water on the sieved fruit and keep in the refrigerator for topping up later. Strain through a fine cloth sieve into a demijohn. Add enough yeast for 1 gallon (4.5 l) according to the instructions on the packet. Seal with an airlock and leave for a few days until the first fierce fermentation has ceased, then top up as required.

Cork or bung down and leave for 6 months.

Siphon into a clean jar and leave until March or April when the bushes are in bloom again.

Bottle into strong dark bottles using wire ties. Keep for another year if you can, but it is very drinkable after a few months when it should begin to sparkle.

I always find that although this is one of the longest wines in the making it is the quickest drunk! It is certainly one of my favourites.

— PEACHES —

Peach Wine

3 lb (1.5 kg) ripe peaches, sliced   2 lb (1 kg) sugar
   and stones removed   Juice of 1 lemon
8 pints (4.5 l) water   ¼ oz (10 g) wine yeast

Place the peaches in a fermentation bucket with 6 pints (3.4 l) of cold water. Bring a further 2 pints (1.2 l) of water to the boil, dissolve the sugar in it and add the lemon juice. Add to the peach pulp. Start the yeast, then add it to the bucket. Cover closely and leave in a warm room to ferment for 4 to 5 days, crushing the pulp daily.

Strain the juice into a demijohn, seal with an airlock and leave to work itself out. Siphon into a clean jar and leave until clear when it can be bottled. Store for at least 6 to 8 months.

·11·
AUTUMN RECIPES

— *GRAIN WINES* —

These include Wheat, Barley, Maize and Rice Wines. Sadly, apart from the Rice Wine, I don't make so much of these nowadays as it is becoming increasingly difficult to buy grain that has not been sprayed with pesticides or other chemicals. Fortunately this is now changing a bit in certain areas and you may be able to buy some organically grown grain.

Grain wines are easy and cheap to make and I call them 'Ted's Whiskies' (because of their whisky colour) after our local blacksmith who loved them, insisting on his daily dose – purporting that it steadied his shoeing arm!

It is important to let these wines mature for at least 2 years or they won't steady anything! I use the same method for all of them and always use demerara sugar. Here are my recipes for Wheat and Rice Wine.

Wheat Wine

8 pints (4.5 l) water
2 lb (1 kg) wheat
3 lb (1.5 kg) demerara sugar
2 lb (1 kg) raisins, washed and
    chopped

Juice of 2 lemons
2 fl oz (50 ml) strong black tea,
    cooled and strained
¼ oz (10 g) wine yeast

Pour the boiling water on to the grain, sugar and raisins in a fermentation bucket and stir to dissolve the sugar. When just warm, add the fruit juice and tea. Start the yeast, then add it to the bucket. Cover closely and leave to ferment for 10 to 14 days, stirring daily.

Strain into a demijohn, seal with an airlock and leave to work itself out.

When the wine begins to clear, siphon into a clean jar, and seal. Leave for a further 3 months until clear. When brilliant, these wines really shine.

Bottle off, and store in a cool place for at least 18 months, preferably much longer.

Rice Wine

8 pints (4.5 l) water
3 lb (1.5 kg) brown rice
3 lb (1.5 kg) demerara sugar
1 lb (450 g) raisins, washed and
   chopped

Juice of 1 lemon
Juice of 1 orange
2 fl oz (50 ml) strong black tea,
   cooled and strained
¼ oz (10 g) wine yeast

Proceed as for Wheat Wine above.

— *ELDERBERRIES* —

I always feel that summer has really arrived when the elder tree is fully in flower and almost over when its berries are ripe. Most years, if the birds allow it, these little black berries litter the lanes so that, after a good walk, you feel you have been well and truly treading the grapes. My love affair with the elderflower extends passionately to these little berries. They have innumerable uses and have been used for medicinal purposes for many years. They are said to induce sleep, cure piles, constipation and chest complaints. All I can vouch for are the soothing properties of the syrup taken in hot water at the onset of a cold or 'flu. So popular was this sweet, warm drink with my own two children that many an 'awful sore throat, mum' was cured immediately! I never questioned their motives, being very aware that prevention is better than cure.

We sometimes picked the lush little berries during the corn harvest and I remember well one extremely hot year when I was quite young our neighbours' binder broke down and I was designated to run up one side of the field behind the mower to throw the cut corn away from that still standing and then be back at my starting corner when it came round again. My little legs were chafed and cut by the sharp stubble and, although very hot and tired, I was still expected to pick some of the ripe elderberries whilst the mower travelled round the rest of the 20-acre field. However, half way down there was a gap in the hedge in which the farmer's dear wife had left me a stone jar of her home-made lemonade. Perhaps the efficacious property of that cool drink was the beginning of my love of home-made wines and cordials.

Don't forget to use dark bottles and jars for your red wines or they will lose their colour.

Elderberry Wine

There are many recipes for this wine. I've given you my most favourite – make as much as you can, but if time is limited (and whose isn't?) the berries freeze well. It will be very popular with family and friends alike. It also makes an excellent base for hot punch or cold cups at party times.

3 lb (1.5 kg) elderberries   *1 teaspoon citric acid*
9 pints (5 l) water   *3 lb (1.5 kg) sugar*
¼ oz (10 g) wine yeast

Strip the berries from the stalks using a dinner fork, weigh them and crush them in a stein or fermentation bucket. Pour on 8 pints (4.5 l) of boiling water and allow to cool. Start the yeast, then add it to the bucket with the citric acid. Dissolve the sugar in the remaining 1 pint (600 ml) of boiling water. Strain the berries through a fine sieve on to the sugar solution. Pour into a dark demijohn and seal with an airlock.

After a few days, when the first vigorous fermentation has subsided, fill the jar to the bottom of the neck with cooled boiled water, replace the airlock and leave until fermentation is complete. This wine is never in a hurry.

Siphon into bottles or clean jars, close tightly and leave for at least 6 months.

MULLED ELDERBERRY WINE   *To make this gracious drink into a delicious warming wine, simply add ½ teaspoon of honey and a pinch of cinnamon per glass and serve warmed, but do not boil. An excellent cure for chilblains.*

Elderberry and Blackberry Wine

You will enjoy making this wine because the colour is wonderful and the blackberries add to the richness, making it more than equal to a good imported burgundy – if we need to make comparisons.

2 lb (1 kg) elderberries	*3 lb (1.5 kg) sugar*
2 lb (1 kg) blackberries	*¼ oz (10 g) wine yeast*
8 pints (4.5 l) water	

Place the fruit in a fermentation bucket. Do be sure to mash up the fruit well before starting as this will speed up the juice extraction. Pour on half the boiling water and stir well. Allow to cool before straining through a fine sieve – don't be tempted to squeeze out that extra drop as this could make your wine cloudy. Add the sugar and enough of the remaining water to make up 1 gallon (4.5 l). Start the yeast, then mix it well into the must. Pour into a demijohn, seal with an airlock and leave to ferment for about 6 months.

Siphon into bottles. This wine can be drunk soon after bottling but does improve with keeping.

THE BERRY AND THE FLOWER   *Old Joe, who farmed near our home, with his two doting, spinster sisters, loved to share his wine – it was always called 'Joe's Wine' but it was his hard-working sisters who actually made it, no doubt, with constant instruction from their brother. He used to argue with me that the only way to make 'proper' Elderberry Wine was to keep it in its cask until the following spring when the flowers were in full bloom, then to add 5 elderflower heads and 1 lb (450 g) of sugar to each 1 gallon (4.5 l) of wine; allow it to stand for 4 to 5 days; siphon off into a clean cask or jar, bung down tightly and leave 'till the flowers be smiling again', as Joe used to say.*

Goodness me, a mere thimbleful was enough to keep the frost at bay, and practically anything else – except Joe's enormous carbuncles. He did suffer so and as I was called upon to dress them and did so very willingly, I was always rewarded with a glass of 'Joe's Berry and Flower'. However, it often crossed my mind that perhaps, just perhaps, it was a little too much of this that was partly to blame for these horrors and that I might be afflicted too. Time, and many of Joe's carbuncles later, proved me wrong and, anyway, this kindly, humorous, old friend's company was in itself a great preserver.

Some Other Elderberry Ideas

As well as wines and cordials, elderberries are absolutely delicious in cooking. I could almost write another book on their innumerable uses! Ever conscious that our present society seems hell bent on producing complex machines and recipes, first to remove most of the vital goodness from our natural fresh resources, then to convert them into synthetic, homogenised, tasteless materials for our consumption, I make no apologies for including a few tips which help me to swim against this tide. Your life and certainly some of your dinner parties will take on a new dimension.

Garnish your jugged beef with a few washed berries – the flavour enhances this rich dish.

Throw a handful into your gravy stock and reduce it to your own taste – gorgeous.

Add a tablespoon to your lamb or mutton casserole – the colour is amazing but you will have to add a pinch more salt than usual.

Elderberry Jam

2 lb (1 kg) elderberries, washed   *1½ lb (750 g) sugar*
½ pint (300 ml) water   *Grated rind and juice of 2*
2 lb (1 kg) apples, peeled, cored   *lemons*
*   and diced*

Place the berries and water in a large saucepan over a low heat. Bruise with a wooden spoon. When the juice is warm, add the apples and 8 oz (225 g) of the sugar. Bring slowly to the boil and simmer gently for about 20 minutes until quite soft. Rub through a fine sieve. Return the pulp to the saucepan. Add the remainder of the sugar and lemon rind and juice. Boil steadily for about 20 minutes or until setting point is reached, pot and cover straight away.

SETTING POINT OF JAM   *You can use a jam thermometer to test the setting point of jam. It has generally reached setting point at 220°F (104°C).*

If you do not have a thermometer, put a teaspoonful of jam on a cold saucer. As the jam cools, a skin forms. If the skin crinkles when you push it with your finger, the jam has reached setting point.

Elder Dessert

This is an unusual and not too sweet dessert – everyone will want the recipe.

8 oz (225 g) elderberries　　　*2 oz (50 g) sugar*
½ pint (300 ml) water　　　*1 tablespoon orange juice*
Juice of 1 lemon　　　*½ pint (300 ml) double cream*

Reserve a few berries for garnish, and simmer the remainder in the water and lemon juice until soft. Sieve them carefully, then return them to the saucepan with the sugar and orange juice. Bring gently to the boil and reduce slightly to syrup consistency. Remove from the heat and allow to cool until just warm, then whisk in the double cream. Pile into glasses and garnish with a bunch of berries.

My Own Elderberry Chutney

Like most pickles, this chutney tastes better after a month or two.

2 lb (1 kg) elderberries without　　　*1 teaspoon ground ginger*
stalks, washed　　　*2 tablespoons demerara sugar*
1 large onion, finely choppped　　　*A good pinch of cayenne*
3 oz (75 g) sultanas, washed　　　*A good pinch of mixed spice*
1 pint (600 ml) vinegar　　　*1 teaspoon mustard seed*
1 teaspoon salt

Put the berries in a large saucepan and bruise them with a wooden spoon. Add the remaining ingredients. Bring to the boil and simmer until thick. Pour into warm jars and cover immediately.

— BLACKBERRY TIME —

One of the greatest joys of making the BBC television series was meeting and becoming friends with so many interesting and knowledgeable people. Molly Harris who, by the way, has also written a book on country winemaking, is a lovely warm woman who, like me, is a 'no fuss' country winemaker. Molly plays Martha, the retired shopkeeper, in *The Archers* radio series.

Molly's Blackberry Wine

It was great fun journeying to Oxfordshire to make Molly's Blackberry Wine – here is her favourite recipe.

Molly reminded us not to pick the low-growing blackberries in case a dog has cocked his leg on them and 'never after 12 October when the devil spits on them'. Not being aware of Molly's warning I have obviously taken many a risk in the past having picked them well into October. Anyway, I have lived to tell the tale and share this old recipe with her.

4 lb (1.75 kg) ripe blackberries	*3 lb (1.5 kg) sugar*
8 pints (4.5 l) water	*¼ oz (10 g) wine yeast*

Roll the berries very gently in a tea towel to remove the dust – Molly never washes them. Place them in a large bowl or bucket and pour the boiling water over them. Cover with a cloth and leave for 3 days, stirring a couple of times a day.

Strain the berries on to the sugar in a fermentation bucket and stir until the sugar has dissolved. Start the yeast, then add it to the bucket. Cover closely and leave for a further 6 days.

Strain the must into a demijohn, top it up with cooled boiled water, and seal with an airlock. Leave to ferment until it has worked itself out.

Rack off into bottles.

Blackberry Preserve

This is a great way of making use of the strained fruit pulp left over from the wine.

4 lb (1.75 kg) Blackberry Wine   FOR EACH I LB (450 G)
pulp   PULP:
                              4 oz (100 g) sugar
                              1 Campden tablet

Put the pulp from the wine mixture through a liquidiser. To each 1 lb (450 g) of pulp add the appropriate amount of sugar. Place in a saucepan and boil until it thickens, stirring well. Add 1 Campden tablet dissolved in a little of the liquor. Seal into jars immediately.

Black and White Blend

My father was exceedingly fond of this blend of rhubarb and blackberries and maintained it was the best cold cure he knew. I think he pretended it was port.

Of course you must think about this one much earlier in the year when the rhubarb wine is in the making. Take the rhubarb wine to the first racking-off stage, then leave it until the first blackberries are ripe.

3 lb (1.5 kg) blackberries   *8 pints (4.5 l) rhubarb wine*
1 pint (600 ml) water

Bring the blackberries and water to the boil in a large saucepan and simmer for 10 minutes. Strain through the finest cloth or sieve that you have. Pour into a clean demijohn and fill up to the neck with the siphoned off rhubarb wine. If there is some over, bottle it and leave it to mature. Seal the demijohn with an airlock and leave for about 3 weeks in case fermentation sets in and then close tightly, leaving it to mature for 6 to 12 months.

— BLAEBERRIES —

Blaeberry, bilberry, hurtleberry, whinberry, truckleberry, whortleberry, known as blueberry in America, this little berry has so many names. In Scotland where we travelled to pick them, the name comes from an old term 'blae' meaning bluish because the berries were once extensively used in dying. Whatever you call them they make a fine wine. I've also included my recipe for Blaeberry Jam as a spoonful in a mug of hot water makes a warming winter drink.

Blaeberry Wine

These berries are rather low in nitrogen so you may need to wait a little longer than usual for the fermentation process to finish.

I haven't made this very often as the little berries are quite scarce but, should you be fortunate enough to find some, you will be well rewarded with a fine, sophisticated wine. Use a dash or two in your chicken casserole to make it worthy of the name I've given it – 'Cock o' the North' – and serve it with a 'wee dram' or two of your wine.

2 lb (1 kg) blaeberries
8 pints (4.5 l) water
2 lb (1 kg) sugar

1 lb (450 g) sultanas, washed
and chopped
Juice of 1 lemon
¼ oz (10 g) wine yeast

Place the washed fruit in a fermentation bucket or stein and cover with 6 pints (3.4 l) of boiling water. When cool, crush the fruit well and leave for 24 hours.

Dissolve the sugar in 2 pints (1.2 l) of boiling water, then allow to cool. Add this to the fruit with the washed and chopped sultanas, and the juice of the lemon. Start the yeast, then add it to the fermentation bucket. Leave to ferment for 4 to 5 days, stirring daily.

Strain into a demijohn and seal with an airlock. Leave to ferment until it has worked itself out.

When the wine starts to clear, siphon into another jar.

When completely clear, siphon the wine into dark bottles and store for at least a year.

Blaeberry Jam

3 lb (1.5 kg) blaeberries   *½ pint (300 ml) water or*
2 lb (1 kg) sugar   *unsweetened apple juice*

Place the ingredients in a large saucepan and bring slowly to the boil, stirring well to dissolve the sugar. Boil rapidly for 30 to 40 minutes or until setting point is reached (see page 77). Whilst still hot, pour into jars and seal immediately.

— MULBERRIES —

'Thou shalt not covet thy neighbour's house, neither his mulberry tree!' I'm sorry, Lord, but I am guilty of the latter . . . Come to think of it, their house isn't bad either!

To have generous friends is a blessing. To have delightfully generous friends who have an old mulberry tree is pure bliss. Edward and Rosemary Pickering are two such friends with an ancient and much revered mulberry tree. It never stirs until all the frosts have dispersed and summer has stored spring away for yet another year. Then, and almost overnight, this wise tree will burst into full bud. In high summer comes the moment captured by John Betjeman in one of his poems:

> 'I lay under the blackening branches
> where the mulberry leaves hung down
> Sheltering ruby fruit globes . . .'

'Ruby fruit globes' describes the berries beautifully.

Mulberry Wine

The wine from these dark rich berries also takes its time to mature – but to what effect! Like the tree, be wise and wait for the bursting forth of the flavour. Oh dear! I'm getting carried away again but do try this old recipe of mine – it does work. And please, please preserve and plant the mulberry again.

8 pints (4.5 l) mulberries
8 pints (4.5 l) water

FOR EACH 8 PINTS (4.5 L)
JUICE:
2 lb (1 kg) sugar
¼ oz (10 g) wine yeast

Place the mulberries in a fermentation bucket and pour on the boiling water. Cover and leave to stand for 2 days. Squeeze the mulberries through a fine sieve or jelly bag. To every 8 pints (4.5 l) of the juice add the appropriate amount of sugar and stir until the sugar has dissolved. Start the yeast, then add it to the must. Pour the must into a demijohn and seal with an airlock. Leave for about 3 to 4 months to work itself out.

When still, siphon into another demijohn or into bottles. Do remember to use dark bottles or tie brown paper round the demijohns to preserve the colour of the wine.

Mulberry Port

This is made by adding brandy to the Mulberry Wine. A small glass of port has wonderful healing properties for most upset tummies, in fact it is a really good pick-me-up at any time. It's very powerful – my father loved it and so do I.

8 pints (4.5 l) Mulberry Wine   1 pint (600 ml) good quality brandy

Rack off the wine a second time, when it should be clear. To each 1 gallon (4.5 l) of wine add 1 pint (600 ml) of brandy. Mix well. Bottle and store for at least a year before drinking.

Mulberry Wine Curd

This is made from the wine pulp and is simply delightful when served with game or poultry; much more interesting than the ubiquitous cranberry sauce we usually serve with our Christmas turkey. The only problem when using the wine pulp is to make sure that it does not continue to ferment. This can be achieved by using a Campden tablet.

2 lb (1 kg) Mulberry Wine pulp   *1 Campden tablet*
2 lb (1 kg) sugar   *Juice of 2 lemons*

Place all the ingredients in a preserving pan and bring slowly to the boil, stirring well. Allow to boil briskly until thick. Pour into jars, cover immediately and leave to cool.

I have found that the Campden tablet prevents mould forming on the top of the curd but don't worry if a skin forms – just remove a thin layer of the preserve and use the rest of the jar, you won't come to any harm. This applies to most preserves when we haven't got cold, dark preserving cupboards and they are affected by heat and light.

Fresh Mulberry Curd

This version uses fresh berries.

2 lb (1 kg) mulberries   FOR EACH 1 LB (450 G)
¼ pint (150 ml) water OR   PULP:
  blackberry cordial OR   *1 lb (450 g) sugar*
  blackcurrant cordial

Place the mulberries in a preserving pan with the water or blackberry or blackcurrant cordial. Simmer until tender. Liquidise or sieve. To each 1 lb (450 g) of pulp add 1 lb (450 g) of sugar. Return to the pan, stir well to dissolve the sugar and boil gently until thickened. Bottle and cover while still warm.

— MORE AUTUMN FRUITS —

Duncan's Rowanberry and Wheat Wine

'Oh Rowan Tree, Oh Rowan Tree,
Thou'll aye be fair tae me.
Entwined thou art wi mony ties
O' hame and infancy.
Oh Rowan Tree.'   Robert Burns

This poem rings very true for me as my father used to sing it to us
as we were gathering the bright berries. It certainly also applies to
Duncan MacDonald – an amazing octogenarian that I had the very
real pleasure of meeting in Inverness. Duncan has been making
country wines for many years, picking all his ingredients from the
hedgerows and fields. My visit to Culloden to collect the rowanberries with Duncan and my winemaking lesson in his garden shed
were among the highlights of my trip. His lovely wife gave me a
true taste of Scottish hospitality.

3 lb (1.5 kg) rowanberries	3 lb (1.5 kg) sugar
8 pints (4.5 l) water	1 tablespoon citric acid
½ pint (300 ml) grape juice	1 teaspoon yeast nutrient
concentrate	¼ oz (10 g) wine yeast
8 oz (225 g) wheat	

Place the berries in a fermentation bucket and pour the boiling
water over them. Stir well and leave to stand for 4 days.

Strain the juice and add the grape juice concentrate, wheat,
sugar, citric acid and yeast nutrient. Start the yeast, then add it to
the bucket. Cover closely and leave to ferment for 16 days.

Strain into a demijohn, seal with an airlock and leave in a warm
place for about 2 to 3 months to work itself out.

When clear, siphon into storage jars or bottles.

Rowanberry Wine

4 lb (1.75 kg) rowanberries   1 oz (25 g) root ginger, bruised
8 pints (4.5 l) water   ¼ oz (10 g) wine yeast
3 lb (1.5 kg) sugar   ½ teaspoon yeast nutrient
Juice of 2 lemons   1 Campden tablet
8 oz (225 g) raisins, washed and
  chopped

Crush the washed rowanberries in a fermentation bucket. Cover with 6 pints (3.4 l) of boiling water and steep for 48 hours.

Bring the remaining 2 pints (1.2 l) of water to the boil and dissolve the sugar in it. When cooled to blood heat, add the lemon juice, washed and chopped raisins and bruised ginger. Start the yeast with the yeast nutrient and add it to the bucket with the Campden tablet. Cover well and leave for 4 days, stirring occasionally.

Strain the liquid off into a demijohn and seal with an airlock. Leave to ferment until it has worked itself out.

When the wine starts to clear, siphon into a clean demijohn.

When clear and bright, siphon into bottles. This wine is at its best the following year when the rowanberries begin to blush again.

Hawthorn Berry Wine

This wine is much, much more successful if you can wait to gather the haws until after a frost or two.

The picking of the haws is a tedious task, but the end result is worth the effort. This is another wine that improves with age, so don't be discouraged if in the first year it is slightly bland – just leave it. Time will give it flavour.

6 lb (2.75 kg) haws   2½ lb (1.25 kg) sugar
8 pints (4.5 l) water   ¼ oz (10 g) wine yeast

Place the haws in a fermentation bucket. Cover with boiling water and leave for at least a week, mashing and pressing each day.

Strain through a fine sieve into a demijohn and stir in the sugar until it has dissolved. Start the yeast, then add it to the jar. Seal with an airlock. Leave in a warm place until it has worked itself out.

Siphon off into a clean jar, cork down and leave for at least 4 months.

Bottle off and store in a cool dark place for 6 to 8 months.

— APPLES —

Now I have to admit that I have become very modern in my approach to apple wine. It is important to extract all the juice from the fruit and some years ago I was given a modern juice extractor. It is wonderful for speeding up the winemaking process. If you are lucky enough to have one, it does take a little while to pulp enough for 1 gallon (4.5 l) of juice but the results are fabulous. Winemaking friends of mine have fruit presses which are also very successful but I have never got round to buying one. With either of them you can pour the cooled juice straight into your fermentation jar, add the yeast and leave to work itself out.

I make the first apple wine from the windfalls – habit really. I used to run my pregnant sows in the orchard and it was always a race to gather the windfalls before they ate them. Not that I begrudge the poor pigs an apple or two but they would gorge themselves into a drunken stupor. My vet bills for hangover cures were quite high – stupid animals!

Apple Wine

Windfalls and crab apples are fine for this delicious wine. The boiling sterilises them and speeds up the fermentation process.

6 lb (2.75 kg) apples
8 pints (4.5 l) water
1 lb (450 g) raisins, washed and
chopped

3 lb (1.5 kg) sugar
¼ oz (10 g) wine yeast

Wash and chop the apples without removing the peel. Place them in a large saucepan with the water. Add the raisins, bring to the boil and simmer for 15 minutes. Pour on to the sugar in a fermentation bucket and stir until the sugar has dissolved. Start the yeast, then add it to the lukewarm must. Cover and leave for 3 days.

Strain through a fine sieve into a demijohn and seal with an airlock. Leave to work itself out. Siphon into jars or bottles. This wine should be left for a few months to mature.

Sister Lucy's Apple Drink

My dear friend Sister Lucy's belief that nothing should be wasted includes the heat in her greenhouse. On a cold day, we prepared her Apple Drink, which was to be stored there in the space just vacated by the tomato plants.

It was a privilege to share her joy in God's bounty. Well over 90 she may be, but her humour and her enthusiasm keep her very young at heart.

Apples
Cold water

Sugar

Using any apples, even quite bruised ones, cut them up, place them in a fermentation bucket and cover them with cold water. Cover and leave to ferment for several days until pulpy.

Strain off the juice and sweeten to taste. Sister Lucy stores this in a plastic barrel which has an air vent. What could be simpler!

— PLUMS —

The variety and types of wines I make from the plum family are many – the early dark ones make light red or rosé wines, luscious Victoria (if you can resist eating them first) will provide bottles of rich sherry-type wine, whilst the golden plums and greengages give a most pleasant dry table wine. Damson, bullace (small, wild plums) and sloe have a quite different flavour and, of course, make wonderful liqueurs.

Most of my recipes for all these lovely wines are very similar, but one important rule applies to all of them. Unless you have managed to stone all the fruit don't add the yeast and ferment without straining the fruit off first, because the kernels may become damaged and can be slightly poisonous, or at least impart a rather bitter taste to the wine. Ripe fruits can be stoned easily but the sloes and damsons are more difficult and must be bruised or pricked to release the juices and flavour of the pulp. Sometimes the fruits may have acquired a bloom, a whitish covering, which could make your finished wine cloudy. Washing them in warm water before stoning or bruising will remove it.

Plum Wine

This recipe is suitable for the early varieties.

5 lb (2.25 kg) plums	*3 lb (1.5 kg) sugar*
8 pints (4.5 l) water	*¼ oz (10 g) wine yeast*

Wash and bruise the plums and place in a fermentation bucket. Pour the boiling water over them. Squeeze the fruit through well washed fingers daily for 4 to 5 days. Strain through a fine sieve on to the sugar, stirring well until it has dissolved. Start the yeast, then add it to the bucket. Pour the must into a demijohn, seal with an airlock and leave to work itself out. Siphon into storage jars or bottles and store for at least 12 months.

— DAMSONS —

The glorious county of Shropshire is renowned for its hedges. I have spent many a contented hour picking blackberries, bullace (a small damson), fruits and nuts of all kinds all round the Wrekin.

Unhappily we have lost too many of these rich larder hedges, sacrificed in the name of better yields from the land. Oh, how short-sighted we are! Not that I blame the farmers. No other industry is so dictated to by governments and consumer demands. When will we realise that our farmers are holding our inheritance in their hands – our land – irreplaceable! Now they are asked to reverse the 'grow more' edict and cultivate tourists instead. How long before we realise how much we need all their inherent skills in caring for our most precious countryside?

Damson Wine

Fortunately, there are still damsons to be found in Shropshire and other parts of the country. Use them to make this rich, full-bodied red wine and then be adventurous enough to make Damson Gin and Damson Port.

It's wonderful to savour a glass of this rich, cheerful wine at the finish of harvesting when the new year's wine is still in the making.

Damsons are quite high in wild yeast so we can use a natural fermentation method.

4 lb (1.75 kg) damsons   *3½ lb (1.5 kg) sugar*
8 pints (4.5 l) water

Place the damsons in a fermentation bucket and bruise them well with your hands or a wooden spoon, taking great care not to crack the kernels because they will impart a very bitter taste. Pour on the boiling water and leave to stand for 48 hours.

Strain the fruit on to the sugar and stir well until the sugar has dissolved. Pour into a demijohn and seal with an airlock. Spontaneous fermentation will take place – just leave the wine to work away until finished.

Strain into a clean demijohn and top up with either cooled boiled damson juice or water. Bung tightly and leave for at least 9 months when it will be very drinkable.

Damson Port

This is made by adding brandy to the Damson Wine.

*8 pints (4.5 l) Damson Wine   1 pint (600 ml) good quality
                                    brandy*

Rack off the wine a second time when it should be clear. To each 1 gallon (4.5 l) of wine add 1 pint (600 ml) of brandy. Mix well. Bottle and store for at least a year before drinking.

— QUINCES —

Quince Wine

3 lb (1.5 kg) ripe quinces
5 pints (2.75 l) water
2 lb (1 kg) sugar
Juice of 2 lemons

8 oz (225 g) sultanas, washed
and chopped
¼ oz (10 g) wine yeast

Peel, core and chop the quinces but keep the peel and cores for later. Put the chopped quinces into a large saucepan with 3 pints (1.75 l) of water and simmer for 25 minutes. Strain the liquor on to the sugar in a fermentation bucket and stir until dissolved. Reserve the pulp for Quince Cheese (see below). Add the remaining 2 pints (1.2 l) of cold water, the lemon juice and washed and chopped sultanas. Start the yeast, then add it to the lukewarm must. Cover and leave to ferment for 3 to 4 days.

Strain into a fermentation jar, top up with cooled boiled water, and seal with an airlock. Leave until it has worked itself out.

Siphon into bottles, then allow to mature in the usual way.

Quince Cheese

Pulp, peel and cores from
    Quince Wine
2 pints (1.2 l) water

FOR EACH I LB (450 G)
    PULP:
1 lb (450 g) sugar

Place the pulp, peel and cores from the Quince Wine in a large saucepan with the water. Bring to the boil and simmer for 30 minutes. Rub through a sieve and then add 1 lb (450 g) of sugar to each 1 lb (450 g) pulp. Bring back to the boil and boil steadily until setting point is reached (see page 77). Seal into warm jars straight away.

·12·
WINTER RECIPES

— *HEDGEROWS* —

Sloe Wine

Sloes are the fruit of the blackthorn tree. Do wait until they have
been well frosted, into late October at the earliest, before picking.

3 lb (1.5 kg) sloes	*8 pints (4.5 l) water*
3 lb (1.5 kg) sugar	*¼ oz (10 g) wine yeast*
8 oz (225 g) sultanas, washed	
and chopped	

Wash the sloes well under cold water and, using a sharp dessert
fork, prick the skins to help release the juices. Place the pricked
sloes in a fermentation bucket with the sugar and sultanas. Pour the
boiling water over them and when cool squeeze the fruit through
well washed fingers to mash the pulp. Start the yeast, then add it to
the bucket. Cover well and leave to ferment on the pulp for 4 to 5
days, stirring daily.

Strain through a fine sieve into a clean fermentation jar and top
up to the neck with cooled boiled water, seal with an airlock and
leave to continue fermenting until it has worked itself out.

Siphon into a clean jar and bung down or bottle it. Leave to
mature for at least a year.

Sloe Gin

Sloe Gin is always popular, and is probably made by more people than most other old country drinks. This simple recipe has always proved very successful but do wait until after the first frost or two before picking the sloes.

1½ lb (750 g) sloes	*2 pints (1.2 l) gin*
4 oz (100 g) sugar	

Stalk, wash and prick the sloes, place in a large screw-top glass jar with the sugar and leave in a warm place for 3 to 4 days.

Add the gin, then store in a dark place for a further 3 to 4 months, occasionally shaking the jar.

Strain off, bottle and store for at least 12 months.

— *A SWEET REWARD* —

So popular is this delicious hedgerow liqueur with family and friends that somehow there is never enough to go round and each year I always resolve to make extra. However, time is usually against me and my grown-up children are now much too busy to spend an evening round the fire 'pricking sloes' – more's the pity!

They were oft times fairly reluctant when faced with umpteen pounds but always succumbed to the offer of their favourite fireside treat as a reward. My mother used the same bribe and it worked – home-made toffee. So just in case some of you have the same problem, and I rather suspect that you might, use these well-tried, fun-to-make treats.

Butter Toffee

4 oz (100 g) butter   2 tablespoons vinegar
8 oz (225 g) granulated sugar   2 tablespoons golden syrup

Melt the butter in a heavy pan over a low heat. Add the remaining ingredients and stir until the sugar is completely dissolved. Bring to the boil, stirring occasionally, until the mixture is golden-brown and a little dropped into a cup of cold water becomes brittle. Pour into a well-greased shallow tin and leave to set.

Treacle Toffee

10 oz (275 g) black treacle   2 teaspoons vinegar
4 oz (100 g) brown sugar   ½ teaspoon bicarbonate of soda
½ oz (15 g) butter

Mix the treacle, sugar, butter and vinegar in a saucepan over a low heat until the sugar is dissolved. Boil without stirring until a little dropped into cold water becomes brittle. Add the bicarbonate of soda, then boil again for 6 to 8 minutes. Pour into a well-greased tin and leave to cool.

My Hedgerow Pudding

My Hedgerow Pudding is inspired by the autumn hedgerows full of colourful fruits simply asking to be used – and it is very inexpensive! This wonderful winter warmer is so unusual and full of country goodness. Over the years it has become a great favourite with family, friends and customers alike. It is absolutely delicious, and will help to keep those colds at bay.

1 lb 13 oz (825 g) blackberries,   3 oz (75 g) demerara sugar
  rose hips, sloes, crab apples   3 oz (75 g) hazelnuts from the
  and hawthorn berries, washed   hedgerows, chopped
Cold water to cover   ½ pint (300 ml) Elderberry
2 lb (1 kg) breadcrumbs   Wine or water

Place all the fruits in a large saucepan and cover them with cold water. Gently bring to the boil and simmer until the apples and sloes are soft and the juice has been extracted from all the fruit. Strain the fruit mixture and return the pulp to the saucepan. Mix together the breadcrumbs, sugar and nuts. Add enough juice to the mixture to make it quite moist, but not wet. Place in a mould or bowl and bake in a moderate oven at 350°F (180°C), gas mark 4 for 40 minutes. Meanwhile return the remaining juice to the pan with the strained fruit, add a little more water or wine and simmer gently to reduce to a syrup. Turn out the pudding and strain the syrup over the top. Serve hot with custard or cream.

— ROSE HIPS —

Now I know that rose hips are getting more scarce in our hedgerows today – I have difficulty in finding enough – but at least they do not hide from us. When the hedges are bare, as in the autumn, you can still find these cheerful, shiny, orange-red hips adorning our lanes. The picking is well worth the effort and the vitamin content is high.

Rose Hip Wine

This is such a useful wine to make. It resembles sherry in colour and taste so, quite apart from drinking it, I use a great deal in my cooking at the restaurant, and for moistening some of the fruit cakes in the bakery. Sometimes it does seem a waste but I cannot bring myself to use the much inferior cooking sherry.

Gather the ripe hips in October or November, preferably after a frost or two which takes out some of the bitterness and helps to achieve this sweet golden wine.

4 lb (1.75 kg) rosehips	*3 lb (1.5 kg) sugar*
Finely peeled rind and juice of	*8 pints (4.5 l) water*
1 lemon	*¼ oz (10 g) wine yeast*

Cut off all the stalks, wash and drain the hips well. If you have a mincer then mince them coarsely or chop them up roughly. Place them in a fermentation bucket with the lemon rind and juice and sugar. Pour on the boiling water and stir well. Start the yeast, then add it to the lukewarm must. Leave to ferment on the pulp for 10 days, stirring daily.

Strain very carefully through one of the finest sieves into a demijohn. Top up to the neck with cooled boiled water and seal with an airlock. Leave to work itself out. This is one of the wines that seem to do much better in a warm store.

When quite still, siphon off into a clean storage jar, top up again with cooled boiled water and leave for 6 to 9 months when it is ready for bottling and drinking.

It is very refreshing served with ice as an aperitif but don't use large glasses as it should be supped before the ice melts!

— VEGETABLES —

Mrs Harding's Potato Wine

Elizabeth Walker, a friend from the village, kindly shared her old recipe for Potato Wine with me. It was given to her in about 1950 when Mrs Harding was 93!

5 lb (2.25 kg) potatoes	*8 oz (225 g) raisins, washed*
8 pints (4.5 l) water	*¼ oz (10g) wine yeast*
3 lb (1.5 kg) sugar	*1 slice of toast*

Place the potatoes and water in a large saucepan. Bring to the boil and boil until soft. Squeeze the liquor well out of them, run it through a sieve and add the sugar. Boil the mixture for 45 minutes. When it is nearly cold add the raisins and the yeast spread on the toast. Cover and leave for 10 days, stirring thoroughly every day.

Strain into a demijohn, seal with an airlock and leave to work itself out. Once fermentation is complete, siphon off into bottles.

My Potato Wine

Never, never use green potatoes and remember that this can be a potent wine – small measures only for this one!

2 lb (1 kg) potatoes
1 lb (450 g) pearl barley
8 pints (4.5 l) water
2 lb (1 kg) demerara sugar

1 lb (450 g) raisins, washed and
chopped
Juice of 2 oranges
1/4 oz (10g) wine yeast

Wash the potatoes well but do not peel them. Chop them up and put them in a large saucepan with the pearl barley and the water. Simmer until the potatoes are just tender. Strain on to the sugar in a fermentation bucket and stir until the sugar has dissolved. When just warm add the chopped raisins and the orange juice. Start the yeast, then add it to the bucket. Cover closely and leave for 7 days, stirring daily.

Strain into a fermentation jar, seal with an airlock and leave to ferment until the wine begins to clear.

Siphon off into a clean jar, seal with an airlock and leave to finish fermenting and until it is completely clear.

Bottle into dark bottles and store. Leave to mature for at least a year – 2 would be better and 3 would be really great – but remember my early warning!

Beetroot Wine

Praise God from whom all mercies flow, and for Dorothy for her flowing songs of praise. Dorothy Dayman-Johns, our talented church organist, choir mistress and her lovely church warden husband certainly don't hide their lights under a bushel, peck, pint or any other vessel. The only 'bottling-up' they practise is with Dorothy's home-made wines and of course even that is shared with everyone. Especially at choir practice – to help relax the vocal cords, as Dorothy puts it.

I made this Beetroot Wine with her. She made me promise to join the choir – as I can't sing a note she must have enormous confidence in her country wine remedies.

Like most root vegetables, this demands old shrivelled beets which have less starch than young beets and make a much better wine. The rich ruby colour will be lost if exposed to too much light, so you must use a dark fermentation jar or cover a clear one with brown paper and do use dark bottles.

4 lb (1.75 kg) old beetroots	*Juice of 2 lemons*
8 pints (4.5 l) water	*¹/₄ oz (10 g) wine yeast*
3 lb (1.5 kg) sugar	

Wash the vegetables well. Slice them without peeling them, and place them in a large saucepan with sufficient water to cover. Bring to the boil and simmer gently for 15 minutes. Strain off the liquid into a fermentation bucket and make up to 8 pints (4.5 l) with the remaining water. Stir in the sugar until it has dissolved. Add the lemon juice. Start the yeast, then add it to the bucket. Cover well and leave to ferment in a warm place for 5 to 6 days, stirring daily.

Strain into a dark fermentation jar, seal with an airlock and leave to work itself out.

When the wine starts to clear, siphon into a clean demijohn and leave to work itself out.

When fermentation has ceased and the wine is bright, bottle and store in a dark place. Like most root vegetable wines it is best left to mature for 2 years.

Carrot Wine

The root vegetable rules applies with this wine as well, so do use old carrots rather than young ones. You won't need as much sugar as usual because of their natural sweetness.

4 lb (1.75 kg) old carrots
8 pints (4.5 l) water
2 lb (1 kg) sugar
Juice of 2 lemons

4 oz (100 g) raisins, washed and
chopped
¼ oz (10 g) wine yeast

Wash and slice the carrots without peeling them and simmer them in the water until just tender. Strain on to the sugar in a fermentation bucket. Add the lemon juice and chopped raisins. Start the yeast, then add it to the lukewarm must. Cover and leave to ferment in a warm place for 7 days, stirring daily.

Strain into a fermentation jar, seal with an airlock and leave to work itself out.

When the wine is clear, siphon off into a clean jar and close with a bung. Leave for about 6 months.

The wine should be ready to bottle in about 6 months but I have found it is far better left for at least a year when it drinks like a fine dry sherry.

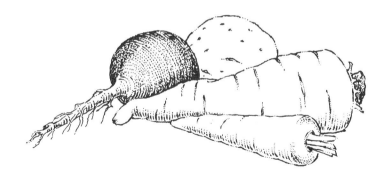

Parsnip Wine

In country wine circles, at least those around our kitchen table, this was known as 'Parson's Wine' rather than parsnip. I have never really known why but I have my suspicions. It is certainly one of the most popular wines, very drinkable, very like a light sherry – no doubt the reason it was considered fit for the parson. The very best wine is made from withered parsnips that have wintered in the ground and have been mellowed by several hard frosts.

4 lb (1.75 kg) old parsnips	8 oz (225 g) sultanas, washed
8 pints (4.5 l) water	and chopped
3 lb (1.5 kg) sugar	4 fl oz (120 ml) strong black tea
Juice of 2 lemons	1/4 oz (10 g) wine yeast

Scrub and peel the parsnips, slice coarsely, and simmer in the water until barely tender. Do not over-boil as the wine will become cloudy. Strain immediately on to the sugar in a fermentation bucket and add the lemon juice, washed and chopped sultanas and the tea. Stir well and leave until lukewarm. Start the yeast, then add it to the lukewarm must. Cover well and leave to ferment for 7 to 10 days, stirring daily.

Strain into a fermentation jar, seal with an airlock and leave to work itself out.

When the wine begins to clear, siphon into a clean jar, seal with an airlock and leave for about 6 months to clear completely.

When clear, siphon into bottles. It is then best left for another year before drinking.

Some years, when we have had early frosts, I have made my Parsnip Wine in December when there were still a few rose hips that the birds could spare. Adding 1 lb (450 g) of these to the parsnip recipe gives the wine a rich autumn glow.

Patrick's Parsnip Wine

Patrick Michael Dransfield is a busy young man living in the heart of Hackney in London who has been making wine since the age of 15, and keeps the tradition going in fine style.

We made Apple, Parsnip, Raisin and Carrot Wines, and out went my theory about not mixing root and fruit.

Patrick's dry sherry-type wine is about as near as you can get to a real sherry without fortifying it. The taste is very similar to that of a good quality dry sherry.

1½ lb (750 g) parsnips
2 lb (1 kg) apples, preferably
   Bramleys
8 pints (4.5 l) water
1 lb (450 g) sultanas, well
   washed to remove the oil
2 lb (1 kg) sugar

½ oz (15 g) pectolase
1 teaspoon yeast nutrient
1 sherry yeast starter bottle
1 oz (25 g) gypsum
½ oz (15 g) tartaric acid or the
   juice of 2 lemons

Scrub and chunk the parsnips and apples. Place the parsnips in a large saucepan, cover with 7 pints (3.9 l) water and boil for 10 minutes. Place the apples and sultanas in a fermentation bucket, and pour over the parsnips, water and all. Dissolve the sugar in 1 pint (900 ml) water and add half to the fermentation bucket. When cool, add the pectolase, yeast nutrient, yeast starter, gypsum and tartaric acid. Cover and ferment on the pulp for 3 days.

Strain off into a demijohn and add the remaining sugar syrup. Ferment down to medium dry and if necessary add a little more sugar in syrup form. Repeat until the alcohol is about 16 per cent, and to test this you will definitely need a hydrometer.

Leave to mature and rack off in the usual manner.

— PUNCHES —

The Bishop

This is inexpensive, not too alcoholic and tastes great.

2 oranges	*2 teaspoons cinnamon*
18 cloves	*1 teaspoon ground ginger*
3 pints (1.75 l) red wine (don't	*1½ pints (900 ml) lemonade*
use one of your best for this)	*8 fl oz (250 ml) brandy*
6 oz (175 g) demerara sugar	*1 lemon, sliced*

Stick one of the oranges with the cloves and bake in a moderate oven at 350°F (180°C), gas mark 4 for 30 minutes to 1 hour. Heat the wine and the baked orange in a saucepan or in the microwave to about blood heat. Add the sugar and spices, stir to dissolve and return to the heat. Add the lemonade and brandy. Pour into a bowl without straining. Slice the remaining orange and garnish the punch with this and the sliced lemon. Keep the punch hot and serve in small glasses.

Hedgerow Punch

This is so simple I don't add spices of any kind. It is better to let the fresh clean taste of the hedgerows come through.

FOR EACH BOTTLE OF
APPLE WINE:
3 fl oz (85 ml) Blackberry Wine

Heat the Apple Wine in a saucepan or in the microwave until piping hot. Add the Blackberry Wine. Serve in small glasses. Savour slowly and you'll very soon feel a warm glow.

Market Day Punch

This will warm the cockles of your heart – and it's easy to remember the recipe. Just think of the three kings of the Orient and spices!

3 oranges
3 lemons
3 oz (75 g) demerara sugar
8 cloves
3 heaped teaspoons grated nutmeg

1 stick cinnamon
3 tablespoons water
Generous 3 pints (1.75 l) cider
3 oz (75 g) rum

Peel the rind from 2 oranges and the lemons very finely and cut into strips. Squeeze the juice and place in the pan with the sugar. Cut the other orange into 8 sections. Stick each section with a clove and sprinkle with nutmeg. Add all these to the pan with the cinnamon and water and heat gently until the sugar dissolves. This can be set aside until you are ready, or even prepared the day before. Half an hour before serving, take out the cinnamon and add the cider. Bring up to really hot but *not* boiling. Add the rum and re-heat a little. Place an orange section in each glass, add the hot cider and serve at once.

— *LONDON* —

It isn't often that I travel up to London, but when I do I love the train journey and my trip with the BBC was no exception. In fact, future trips will never be the same. For years I have wondered just what city dwellers did with all the fruits and flowers grown in their gardens and allotments – did they make wine with the elder that I could see from the train? Some living in those high tower blocks perhaps didn't have gardens or allotments – how did they manage?

Well now I know. I've seen the wonderful markets, sampled some of the huge variety of roots, fruits and flowers on sale, at fair prices too. And I've met some wonderful people who do make the most of the good life even in a tiny London flat – great stuff. I'll never again think that city dwellers can't find the raw materials. Oh, I know it's much more fun to walk the lanes and pick everything fresh, but it can be time-consuming and no one has any time to spare these days, more's the pity. And of course I don't have to live in a concrete jungle, but London is still full of wonderful green areas and hundreds of lovely trees, not to mention truly enterprising folk making the most of the markets.

Shirley and Germaine are two such souls. They shared with me some of their Caribbean traditions handed down from grandmother to mother to daughter – what's new?!

I loved this Sorrel Punch; not sorrel as we know it but a plant grown in Trinidad called rosella.

These two lovely sisters gave me the recipe and I'm going to try it. I have often thought that all the ethnic restaurants springing up everywhere have brought us the world on our plate. Now we can broaden our experience with the world in our glass, mixing country traditions with that most important ingredient of loving friendship.

Sorrel Punch

This is made from the sepals of an annual plant called rosella (sorrel). It is a traditional Christmas drink in Trinidad and can be made with both fresh and dried sorrel.

3 pints (1.75 l) water
3 oz (75 g) dried sorrel
3-in (7.5-cm) piece of dried
*   orange peel*
6 cloves

1 lb (450 g) sugar
6 tablespoons rum (preferably
*   Trinidad rum) (optional)*
1 teaspoon Angostura bitters

Boil the water and pour it over all the ingredients except the rum and Angostura bitters in a fermentation bucket. Allow to cool, cover loosely and leave for 2 to 3 days.

Strain, then leave for another 2 days.

Strain again through a fine sieve lined with cheesecloth and add the rum and Angostura bitters. The rum can be omitted for a non-alcoholic drink. Stir. Serve in chilled glasses with ice-cubes.

If you can't wait this long, it can be strained off and drunk after 2 days.

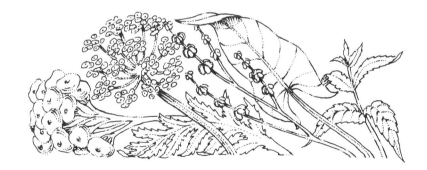

·13·
YEAR-ROUND RECIPES, SYRUPS AND CORDIALS

— *CITRUS FRUITS* —

Citrus Wine

Juice of 3 lemons

Juice of 3 grapefruits

Juice of 3 sweet oranges

2 lb (1 kg) sugar

5 pints (2.75 l) water

8 oz (225 g) raisins, washed and
  chopped or liquidised

¼ oz (10 g) wine yeast

Wash the fruit well and squeeze out all the juice. This should give about 1 pint (600 ml). Dissolve the sugar in 3 pints (1.75 l) of boiling water in a fermentation bucket and add the remaining 2 pints (1.2 l) of cold water, the washed and chopped raisins and the fruit juice. Stir well and allow to cool. Start the yeast, then add it to the lukewarm must. Cover well and leave in a warm place to ferment for 3 to 4 days.

Strain through a fine sieve into a demijohn and top up to the neck with cooled boiled water. Seal with an airlock and leave to work itself out.

Siphon off, bottle and allow to mature in the usual way.

Three Fruit Marmalade

Squeezed fruit from Citrus Wine *3 pints (1.75 l) water*
2 lemons *3 lb (1.5 kg) sugar*

Squeeze the juice from the 2 fresh lemons and keep aside. Tie the pips from all the fruit in a muslin bag and slice the peel to the thickness you like. Put the peel and bag of pips in a pan with 2 pints (1.2 l) of water and simmer for about 90 minutes or until the peel is soft. Remove the pips, add 1 pint (600 ml) of water, the lemon juice and sugar and stir to dissolve. Boil steadily until setting point is reached (see page 77) and seal in warm jars straight away. This makes about 4 lb (1.75 kg) of marmalade.

Orange Wine

12 Seville oranges *3½ lb (1.5 kg) sugar*
8 pints (4.5 l) water *¼ oz (10 g) wine yeast*

Thinly pare the peel of the oranges without removing any of the white pith. Cut it up and put it in a fermentation bucket. Cut the oranges in half, squeeze out all the juice and strain it into the bucket. Pour the boiling water over the peel, stir well and leave for 3 days, stirring daily to extract all the flavour.

Strain off the peel and stir the sugar into the liquor. Start the yeast, then add it to the liquor. Pour into a fermentation jar, seal with an airlock and leave in a warm place to work itself out.

Siphon off, bottle and mature as usual.

Phil Hardy's Three-Carton Wine

As I've mentioned before, one of the greatest joys of working with the BBC has been meeting interesting, lovely and kind people like Phil Hardy, his lovely wife, Rose, and to see their new baby boy, Sam, soon after his birth. Phil, in the age-old tradition, made some port wine to be drunk on Sam's twenty-first birthday. I hope to be there to share in the celebration and, of course, taste that port!

Phil made this modern Three-Carton Wine. I find the anomaly of no additives in the carton, only to see him use more additives than I've ever known, never mind used, very strange. How I teased him about that! But I have to admit that the wine was good.

3 × 1-l (1¾-pint) cartons fruit juice (any combination – Phil uses apple and grape)
MUST NOT CONTAIN ANY ARTIFICIAL PRESERVATIVE OR SWEETENER

1 teaspoon Bentonite
1 teaspoon pectolase
¼ teaspoon Minavit yeast nutrient

2 teaspoons tartaric acid (depending on the acidity of the fruit)
¼ teaspoon liquid tannin
17 oz (480 g) sugar dissolved in 1 pint (600 ml) boiled water
¼ oz (10 g) wine yeast
2 teaspoons sulphite solution

Place all the ingredients, except the yeast and sulphite, in a demijohn. Start the yeast, then add it to the demijohn and shake well. Seal with an airlock and leave in a warm place for 3 or 4 days.

Top up to the neck of the demijohn with cooled boiled water, seal with an airlock and leave to ferment for about 3 to 6 weeks.

Siphon the wine into a clean demijohn, add 1 teaspoon of sulphite, seal again and leave for about 8 weeks.

Siphon off again and add another teaspoon of sulphite to the wine. Seal and leave to clear for 3 to 6 weeks.

When the wine is clear, bottle it up. It is better if kept in the bottles for about 6 months before drinking.

— *APRICOTS* —

Apricot Wine

8 oz (225 g) dried apricots
6 pints (3.4 l) water
2 lb (1 kg) sugar
1 teaspoon tartaric acid

½ teaspoon citric acid
4 fl oz (120 ml) strong black tea,
  cooled and strained
¼ oz (10 g) wine yeast

Wash the fruit well to remove the oils and soak overnight in 3 pints (1.75 l) of water. Chop up the apricots and simmer in the same water for 25 minutes. Strain the juice on to the sugar in a fermentation bucket and stir to dissolve the sugar. Make up to 6 pints (3.4 l) with cooled boiled water and add all the other ingredients except the yeast. Start the yeast, then add it to the lukewarm must. Pour the must into a fermentation jar and seal with an airlock. Allow to work itself out, topping up occasionally in the usual way.

Siphon into bottles and allow to mature.

Apricot Chutney

Pulp from Apricot Wine
1 lb (450 g) apples, peeled,
  cored and chopped
1 pint (600 ml) vinegar
Pickling spices
4 oz (100 g) raisins, washed

4 oz (100 g) sultanas, washed
1 teaspoon salt
2 cloves of garlic, finely chopped
1 lb (450 g) brown sugar
Finely grated rind and juice of 1
  lemon

Place the apricot pulp, chopped apples and ½ pint (300 ml) of vinegar in a large saucepan. Add the pickling spices tied in a muslin bag. Bring to the boil and simmer for 10 minutes. Add the washed raisins and sultanas, salt, chopped garlic and the remaining vinegar. Simmer for another 15 minutes, then add the brown sugar and the lemon rind and juice. Boil gently for about 45 minutes until the chutney is nice and thick. Remove the bag of pickling spices and seal immediately into warm jars.

You can make a Peach Chutney in the same way using the pulp from the Peach Wine on page 71.

— SOFT DRINKS —

Old-Fashioned Ginger Beer

I've had many a laugh on the term 'ginger beer plant' and have often been asked for a cutting. Here's the secret – you make a starter and go from there. Here's how.

FOR THE 'STARTER':
½ oz (15 g) yeast
3/4 pint (450 ml) warm water
2 teaspoons ground ginger
2 teaspoons sugar

TO FEED THE 'PLANT':
6 teaspoons ground ginger
6 teaspoons sugar

TO FLAVOUR THE END
RESULT:
1½ lb (750 g) sugar
2 pints (1.2 l) water
Juice of 2 lemons

TO DILUTE:
5 pints (2.75 l) water

Mix together the starter ingredients in a glass jar with a lid. Stir well, cover and leave in a warm place for 24 hours (a sunny windowsill is fine).

Feed with 1 teaspoon of ground ginger and 1 teaspoon of sugar daily.

After 7 days, strain the 'plant' through a fine sieve.

To flavour the drink, dissolve the sugar in warm water. Add the lemon juice and the liquid from the 'plant'.

Dilute with 5 pints (2.75 l) of water. Mix well and bottle in a corked bottle for at least 7 days to mature.

This drink is equally delicious served iced with a sprig of mint or gently mulled with a dash of Blackcurrant or Elderberry Rob.

Old-Fashioned Lemonade

This makes about 6 to 8 glasses.

3 lemons	*Ice*
3 tablespoons brown sugar	*A few sprigs of mint*
2 pints (1.2 l) water	*Slices of lemon to garnish*

Wipe the lemons and place them on a plate before slicing so that you save all the juice. Put them into a jug with the sugar. Pour on the boiling water and leave to steep for at least 2 hours; it can be 24 hours. Strain and serve in glasses with ice, mint and slices of lemon.

Mintade

This is a delicious, pale green drink – very refreshing served with mint chocolate biscuits.

3 lemons	*2 pints (1.2 l) water*
A few crushed mint leaves	*A few sprigs of mint*
3 tablespoons brown sugar	

Wipe and slice the lemons as you did for the Lemonade, saving the juice. Put them into a jug with the crushed mint leaves and the sugar. Pour on the boiling water and leave to steep for at least 2 hours. Strain and serve in glasses with sprigs of mint.

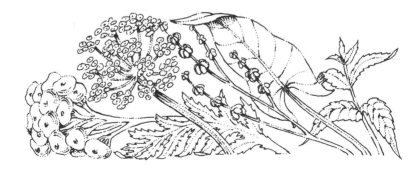

— CORDIALS —

I want to include a few of my most used recipes for these healthy, non-alcoholic drinks in the hope of giving inspiration to use more natural products to quench our thirsts, especially those of our growing youngsters.

Remember they will not keep for much more than a year and all bottles and tops must be sterilised by immersing in boiling water for 20 minutes. After filling the bottles with the syrup to ½ in (1 cm) below the bottom of the screw-top, screw down the top then give it a half turn to loosen it slightly. Stand the bottles in a double saucepan or fish kettle up to their necks in cold water. Bring slowly to the boil, then simmer for 20 minutes. Allow to cool slightly. Carefully lift out the bottles, avoiding cool surfaces, and screw down tightly. Leave to cool, then label the bottles. In order to seal the bottles completely I wrap cling film round the tops before storing them in a cool dark cupboard. Cordials will keep till the fruits are ripe again the following year but should be drunk quickly once the bottle has been opened.

This sounds a lengthy process, but it is really quite simple and well worth the effort.

Lemon and Ginger Cordial

2 oz (50 g) root ginger, bruised   *2 pints (1.2 l) water*
1 lemon, thinly sliced   *2 lb (1 kg) brown sugar*

Boil the ginger and lemon in the water for 45 minutes. Make up to 2 pints (1.2 l) with boiled water. Remove from the heat, add the sugar and stir until it has dissolved.

Bottle, seal and store.

Mum's Cold Cure

This is a wonderfully soothing hot toddy. Use a tablespoon of cordial in a tumbler of hot water – gosh it's good!

1 lb (450 g) blackberries   *1 lb (450 g) sugar*
1 pint (600 ml) white wine   *8 oz (225 g) clear honey*
  vinegar

Wash the fruit, then place it in a large bowl and crush it well. Pour over the wine vinegar, cover and leave for 1 week, pressing the fruit daily.

Strain the liquid into a saucepan and add the sugar and honey. You can use the pulp to make a blackberry pie. Bring the liquid slowly to the boil, then simmer for 5 to 10 minutes. Leave to cool, then bottle, seal and store.

Elderberry Rob

Rob is the old name for a cordial. One to 2 tablespoonfuls in hot water taken at the onset of a chill or cold is wonderfully healing. If you haven't time to make the Rob, use a good teaspoon of the Elderberry Jam in a mug of hot water. Both are better by far than so many of the modern proprietary cold remedies.

1 lb (450 g) fresh elderberries,
  crushed
1 lb (450 g) brown sugar

Simmer the fresh, washed, crushed berries with the sugar until the consistency of syrup. Pass through a fine sieve and then bottle.

Most proprietary brands of blackcurrant cordial have less than 5 per cent pure blackcurrant.

Blackberry Cordial

This is a must for every medicine cabinet. It makes a very soothing healing drink for sore throats and feverish colds. My children love to drink it on cold days diluted with an equal amount of warm water or to taste.

4 lb (1.75 kg) blackberries

FOR EACH 1 PINT (600 ML) JUICE:
1 lb (450 g) brown sugar
¼ oz (10 g) grated nutmeg
1 clove
1 teaspoon brandy (optional)

Squeeze the juice from the blackberries. Measure the juice and add the appropriate amounts of sugar, nutmeg and cloves. Bring to the boil and simmer gently for 10 to 15 minutes. Allow to cool. I actually add a good teaspoon of brandy to each 1 pint (600 ml) just before bottling, but this is only a matter of taste and is not essential. Bottle and store in a cool cupboard.

Other Fruit Cordials

Simply substitute other fruits and follow the Blackberry Cordial recipe to make:

Blackcurrant Cordial   Redcurrant Cordial
Strawberry Cordial   Raspberry Cordial

– all delicious and much healthier than proprietary brands.

Elderflower Cordial

This is a must for every household concerned about what is in some of the so-called 'whole fruit juice' cordials on the shelves today. Serve this to children and adults alike as a real thirst quencher, knowing it to be truly wholesome. I journeyed to south Somerset to meet the delightful Pizzie family and to share their recipe. The boys, Matthew and Ben, make it themselves so they certainly won't forget mum's recipe, will they! How lucky they are to have an elderflower orchard!

Sally Pizzie freezes this into small, plastic, ice cube bags so that she has a permanent store and need only bring out the exact quantities needed – an idea that I have taken up for all my cordials – and marvellous for ensuring a winter supply to help fend off the colds.

3 pints (1.75 l) water   *2 oz (50 g) tartaric acid*
3 lb (1.5 kg) brown sugar   *4 oranges, sliced*
25 elderflower heads   *1 lemon, sliced*

Place everything in a bucket and leave for 24 hours. Strain. Bottle or freeze.

Dilute to taste. What could be easier?

— SYRUPS —

Syrups can be made from all the currant fruits, the berries, plums, damsons, rosehips, citrus – in fact, almost any fruit. They can be diluted as drinks, poured over ice-cream or stirred into yoghurt. I use a standard recipe for all of them. The only adjustment is the amount of water needed with the different fruits. The fruit must always be ripe.

1 lb (450 g) ripe fruit, washed (use juice and finely sliced peel only for citrus fruits)
No water required for strawberries, raspberries, citrus fruits

¼ pint (150 ml) water for blackberries, blackcurrants, loganberries
OR ½ pint (300 ml) water for stone fruits
OR 1 pint (600 ml) water for rose hips
8 oz (225 g) sugar

Place the fruit in a heavy saucepan and crush or chop finely, depending on the type. Remove the stones from the plums etc. Add the water (if using), heat gently and cook for 1 hour (cook rosehips for 20 minutes), stirring and pressing the fruit occasionally.

Strain through a fine mesh sieve or jelly bag. Make up the liquid to 1 pint (600 ml) with boiled water. Stir in the sugar and heat gently until it dissolves, but do not boil the liquid or you will have a pleasant thin jam!

Bottle, seal and store as for cordials.

Instead of bottling syrups, you can freeze them in ice cube trays, then take out exactly the quantity you want.

·14·
DAVID WEBB'S WINES

It would be almost impossible to place in order of merit all the wines that I've had the fun of tasting during our four seasons of filming *Fruity Passions*, but very near the top of the shortlist must be some wonderful samples from David Webb at Buckfastleigh. David's wines are absolute proof of my theory that country wines reflect the characters of the makers.

His are very individual, nonconformist and warm-hearted – just like the man himself. He has established his own simple methods using up everything available from the land and even greengrocer's throwaways, and most successfully too. Not wishing in any way to detract from David's skills as a winemaker, I am certain that the quality of his own well water is a contributory factor to the success of the final products.

Here are David's recipes – just as he gave them to me.

Cold Fermentation Method

All the wines are cold fermented. Just leave to brew at ordinary room temperature. Will take longer but that doesn't matter. Rack if large sediment builds up or when clear. Make back up to a gallon with some of the previous year's wine. Same variety if available, or similar if not. Fermentation could take anything from 3 months to 2 years.

Only drink when perfectly clear.

Dandelion Wine

4 pints (2.25 l) dandelion
*   flowers*
8 pints (4.5 l) boiling water
3 lb (1.5 kg) sugar

1 teaspoon citric acid
2 teaspoons wine yeast compound
*   (I use Boots')*

Pick dandelion heads. No stalks. Don't bother about pulling petals from green calices. Put whole heads in a bucket. Pour on a gallon of boiling water. Steep for a while until you remember – 4 days maybe.

Strain on to the sugar. Do not press pulp. Only drain pulp naturally. Stir vigorously to dissolve sugar. Stir in a teaspoon of acid. Sprinkle on 2 teaspoons of yeast compound. It should start working within 24 hours. Check to see if started working.

Mayflower Wine

Pick out a hawthorn bush with main stem no thicker than your arm with flowers just starting to fall. Lay clean sheets on ground under bush. Shake the living pygmies out of the bush. All the petals will fall on to the sheets. Pick out and throw away the majority of the leaves which fall. I am not too fussy, I leave the odd bug and caterpillar in. Gather about 4 pints (2.25 l) of petals. Pour on a gallon of boiling water. Steep and continue as Dandelion Wine.

Lettuce Wine

At least 2½ lb (1.25 kg) lettuce, including at least 1–1½ lb
(450–750 g) red lettuce to give a rosé colour

8 pints (4.5 l) water   1 teaspoon citric acid
3 lb (1.5 kg) sugar   2 teaspoons wine yeast compound

Boil the lettuce in water. Simmer for a while. Strain on to the
sugar. Stir up. Add acid. Sprinkle on yeast.

Rose Hip Wine from Species Roses

3 lb (1.5 kg) species rose hip   3 lb (1.5 kg) sugar
*   husks   1 teaspoon citric acid*
8 pints (4.5 l) water   2 teaspoons wine yeast compound

Let the greenfinches pick open the hips and eat the seeds. Then pick
what remains of the hips. Wash hips. Pour boiling water on to hips
and sugar. When cool, add acid and yeast. Ferment on pulp for
about a week. Strain – do not press – and continue fermentation.

Parsnip Wine

Whenever you have parsnips for dinner, save water they have
boiled in until you've got a gallon (can be stored in freezer until
you've got enough).

8 pints (4.5 l) parsnip juice   1 teaspoon citric acid
3 lb (1.5 kg) sugar   2 teaspoons wine yeast compound

Stir up juice and sugar. Add acid and yeast as usual.

·15·
CLUBS AND COMPETITIONS

There are winemaking clubs and circles all over Britain, as well as in Canada, Australia and quite a few in the Netherlands. Not to be confused with wine tasting or appreciation societies (although a lot of tasting and appreciating goes on!), they offer friendly practical advice and a chance to compare the fruits of your labours with others. This last factor – the tasting and comparing – can be off-putting for a newcomer who has never been to a wine circle. Fear not. In making the *Fruity Passions* television series, we visited tiny village circles, who met in each other's homes, and large urban groups with a range of speakers. They could not have been more friendly and are constantly welcoming newcomers to winemaking.

Most circles meet once a month and there is usually a practical demonstration or speaker, followed by an informal tasting and sharing of wines. Everyone brings a bottle of their home-made wine and a small tasting glass and you all swap recipes and tips. Some of the larger groups have special classes for beginners and there is often a monthly competition for, say, the best dessert wine or the best wine from tinned peaches! If the speaker has given a particular recipe, the whole group might make it at home and there will be a competition a year later to judge the results.

The present wine circle movement in England started in Andover in 1953. Others sprung up across the south, and in 1959 the first Amateur Winemakers' Festival was held in Hertford. Today there are a number of regional festivals and shows, where competition is keen and judging is very strict. The National Guild of Wine Judges and Beermakers have a rigorous entrance exam and the judges travel far and wide to give talks and award prizes. At the

Wales and West Show, which we filmed in Somerset, and the annual National Show, there are literally thousands of bottles ranged along great long tables. The bottles have to be clear glass with a regulation cork stopper and a label in *exactly* the right place with just an entry number to witness the winemaker.

The judging of the wines can take a whole morning and the contestants are not allowed into the hall while it is taking place. Each judge has a steward (often a would-be judge in training) who pours the wine and makes notes on the judge's comments. Points are given for colour, clarity, bouquet and so on, then the wines are thoroughly tasted, but not swallowed, of course (there may be a hundred entries in a large class!). The top dozen or so bottles are tasted again, the certificates and rosettes awarded and the identity of the maker revealed.

At most of the large shows, there is a very informative session called 'Judges at the Bar' where you can ask the judge of a particular section to refer back to his or her notes and give an opinion on your wine. How could it have been improved and what should you try to avoid next time? But the festivals are not all point-scoring and prize-winning. They are usually held over a weekend and there is just as much socialising as there is scientific tasting – especially when judging of the bottles is over and the contents consumed!

It is interesting that while most wines at these festivals are still classed by their colour and purpose, 'Table Red' or 'Social White', for example, the Country Wine classes, which tend to go by the main ingredient, appear to be on the increase. Perhaps the movement is turning back to elderflowers and blackberries and away from tins of grape juice concentrate. Whatever school you follow and whether you are highly competitive or just call into your village circle for a drink and a chat, you are bound to improve your winemaking and you will certainly find good cheer and company. If you do not know where to find your nearest circle, then your local library should have the information – or ask in your nearest home-brew shop. Happy winemaking!

GLOSSARY

Here are brief explanations of some of the words used in the book, as well as others which you may come across in home-brew stores or at wine circles.

AIRLOCK *A simple glass or plastic twisted tube used to exclude the air from the fermenting ingredients while allowing carbon dioxide to escape. The airlock should always be kept half full of water.*

AMYLASE *A starch-destroying enzyme.*

BENTONITE *A clay mineral used to clear cloudy wine.*

BUNG *A rubber stopper used to seal a fermentation jar. Some have a hole in the centre to hold an airlock.*

CAMPDEN TABLET *Sodium metabisulphite tablet used for sterilising equipment.*

DEMIJOHN *A large vessel in clear or brown glass for secondary fermentation of wine.*

FERMENTATION *The process in which yeast feeds on sugar to produce alcohol and carbon dioxide.*

FERMENTATION BUCKET *White plastic bucket with lid suitable for fermenting on the pulp.*

FERMENTATION JAR See *demijohn.*

FERMENTATION LOCK See *airlock.*

FERMENTING ON THE PULP *Starting fermentation of a sugar, fruit or flower and yeast mixture before straining off the juice to continue fermentation.*

FINING *Clearing cloudy wine.*

HYDROMETER *An instrument for measuring the specific gravity of wine.*

LEES *The sediment which forms at the bottom of wine during fermentation or maturing.*

MATURATION *The time during which the flavour of the wine improves after fermentation.*

MEAD *Wine made from honey.*

MUST *The fruit, sugar and water mixture which is fermented with yeast to form wine.*

OXIDATION *Exposure of wine to air, which can make it discolour.*

PECTIN *A substance in some fruits which can cause hazes in wine.*

PECTINASE *A substance used to prevent pectin hazes.*

PECTOLAZE *See pectinase.*

RACKING *Siphoning clear wine from the sediment.*

SODIUM METABISULPHITE *A chemical used to sterilise equipment.*

SPECIFIC GRAVITY *The weight of must or wine compared with the same volume of water.*

YEAST *An organism which feeds on sugar solutions to produce alcohol and carbon dioxide.*

YEAST NUTRIENT *Mineral salts, vitamins and other substances which encourage yeast cells to grow and multiply.*